The Art of Dying Before You are Dead

OrangeBooks Publication

1st Floor, Rajhans Arcade, Mall Road, Kohka, Bhilai, Chhattisgarh 490020
Website: **www.orangebooks.in**

First Edition, 2026

ISBN: 978-93-6554-615-6

Price: Rs. 499.00

Printed in India

THE ART OF DYING *Before* YOU ARE DEAD

Why Meaning is Optional and Living is Enough ?

UMESH SHRIVASTAVA

OrangeBooks Publication
www.orangebooks.in

Preface

Dear Reader, You Poor Fool.

First of all, I want to congratulate you.

You've either made a terrible mistake by picking up this book, or a glorious one. Either way, the outcome is delightfully pointless, and I deeply admire your commitment to wasting your time in such a poetic way.

This is not a self-help book. You will not find 7 habits, 12 rules, or 101 affirmations here. In fact, you will find very little help at all, mostly because you don't need it. Not because you're already whole and perfect (don't flatter yourself), but because there's ultimately nothing to be helped from. The disease, dear reader, is imaginary. So is the cure. And so, hilariously, is the one seeking either.

What you hold in your hands is not a guide to life. It is a slow striptease of its absurdity. A lovingly written slap in the face to every illusion you've carefully moisturised and called "truth." You may be hoping for answers, but answers are what got you into this mess in the first place.

Here's a little secret

You're already dead.

But you just haven't stopped breathing yet.

This book is about learning the art of dying before you're dead. Not the dramatic kind, with coffins and violins, no. This is the quieter, more rebellious kind. The death of your seriousness. Your precious self-image. Your belief that the universe is a customer service desk, and that meaning is just one more refund request away.

This is a book for those who've grown tired of pretending. For those who sense that the game is rigged, the rules are made up, and the prizes are cheap plastic trinkets. But instead of despairing, you laughed. Or at least, smirked. And that, my friend, is the beginning of your liberation.

You will not be convinced of anything here. I am not a guru, and you are not a disciple. This is not a cult. (Although if it were, we'd probably have better snacks.) I offer no enlightenment, no salvation, and certainly no refunds.

What I offer, if anything, is a mirror.

One that distorts nothing and flatters no one.

Look in it, or don't.

Laugh, or weep.

Read on, or burn this book and use the ashes to season your next meal.

It's all the same to me.

But if you *do* continue… know this:

Something inside you *will* die.

And that may be the best thing that has ever happened to you.

With irreverent love,

A fellow corpse-in-progress

Synopsis

The Art of Dying Before You are Dead

The Art of Dying Before You're Dead is not a self-help book; it is a self-destruction book, in the best possible sense. Unabashedly, it asks the one question no bestselling guru wants you to face: What if everything you've been chasing, success, happiness, even God, is just a well-decorated illusion?

Through nine provocative chapters, the book dismantles modern life's greatest myths: the cult of productivity, the fetish of meaning, the commodification of spirituality, and the illusion of success. Each illusion is not merely mocked but stripped bare, revealing the absurdity of the stories we tell ourselves. Whether it is a God reduced to a supernatural shopkeeper or enlightenment packaged like a subscription box, the book tries to uncover uncomfortable rational truths in a satirical tone.

And yet, beneath the sarcasm lies a serious invitation: to die before you die. Not in the literal sense, but in the deeper way mystics hinted at and philosophers whispered about, the death of ego, of false identities, of secondhand truths. To see the machinery of illusions collapse, and in that collapse, to stumble into freedom.

Drawing from a lifetime of reading, years in business boardrooms, and the raw honesty of the classroom, I try to bring a voice that is irreverent yet empathetic, critical yet deeply human. This is not a book that flatters the reader; it confronts them. It does not hand out steps to success; it hands you a mirror and dares you to look.

At its core, *The Art of Dying Before You're Dead* is a survival manual for those who are wise enough to know they are mortal, and stubborn enough to laugh anyway.

Acknowledgement

I wish to dedicate this book to myself, because let's be honest, no one else was going to do it with the enthusiasm I deserve. I have been outrageously fortunate to read, write, think, overthink, misunderstand, comprehend, and then confidently disseminate those misunderstandings as wisdom. This book exists because I stubbornly refused to shut up, and for that alone, I deserve a small ceremony in my honour.

And yet, in a rare moment of generosity, I also dedicate this book to my future generations, who, I sincerely hope, will be far more evolved than I am. May they read this someday, smile at my naïve brilliance, forgive my philosophical detours, and think, *"Poor guy... at least he tried."*

If they surpass me, good.

If they don't, even better, I get to feel superior long after I'm gone.

Either way, this dedication stands.

To me.

And to them.

In that order.

Table of Contents

Chapter - 1

Life Slid into My DMs

I remember the time when my life was coming apart like a bad PowerPoint presentation, one slide crashing after another. I was in the middle of a PhD, a divorce, and an existential meltdown, all happening on alternate days just to keep things interesting. My PhD coordinator demanded journal publications while the court demanded my presence. I was hanging by a thread so thin it could have doubled as dental floss. It was absurd, painful, and weirdly comic, like watching your own house burn while giving a TED Talk about fire safety. I could not concentrate on anything, and it irritated me. Plus, I had taken the biggest decision of my life, to pursue a four-year residential FPM program. It wasn't a casual "let's see how it goes" decision. It was a leap into a furnace that promised rigour, sweat, and rejection in generous doses.

At first, I thought I was signing up for an academic degree. I was wrong. Somewhere between the deadlines and the self-doubt, I began to realise that an FPM isn't a qualification, it's a spiritual stripping. It humbles you, breaks your pride, mocks your intelligence, and then politely asks for another draft. It takes everything from you until the only thing left is surrender. But within that exhaustion, something shifts. You begin to feel grateful for the tiniest things: a full night's sleep, a quiet cup of tea, a breath that isn't heavy with deadlines. The world doesn't change, but your lens does. And if it doesn't, you've probably learned nothing. You might even need another PhD.

Somewhere in that quiet shift, I began to see patterns, not just in my life, but in Life itself. It was as if, while I was busy dissecting research problems, Life had been quietly studying me back. And one day, it decided to make the first move. That's when Life, that mysterious prankster, slid into my DMs. Not literally, of course, but it felt that personal. It whispered to me, not seductively, but conspiratorially. Life wasn't flirting; it was ranting. It was tired of us humans and our endless demands. We treat Life like a customer service executive on hold. "I need purpose." "I need validation. I need a tracking number for my destiny." Life sighed, and I swear I could hear the weariness in its voice.

That's when I saw it, the joke we never get. We crave meaning like addicts, terrified of silence, of emptiness. We swipe right on distractions, desperate for confirmation that we still exist. But Life isn't a puzzle to solve, it's a mystery to live. I had spent years trying to "understand" it, to make sense of its absurdity. But the moment I stopped trying, it began to make sense on its own. The truth is, the only temporary worth having is Life. Death is punctual and consistent; you never have to chase it. Life, on the other hand, is slippery. It arrives uninvited, overstays its welcome, and leaves without notice. The challenge is learning how to exist in that small, ridiculous gap between arrival and departure without losing your mind.

I started noticing how nature handles existence. The river flows because it must, not because it seeks approval. The flower blooms unseen, and the tree sheds without a motivational quote. There is no cosmic scoreboard. No celestial accountant tracking who lived meaningfully. Everything just… happens. And that's the beauty of it, things are happening, and yet nothing really is.

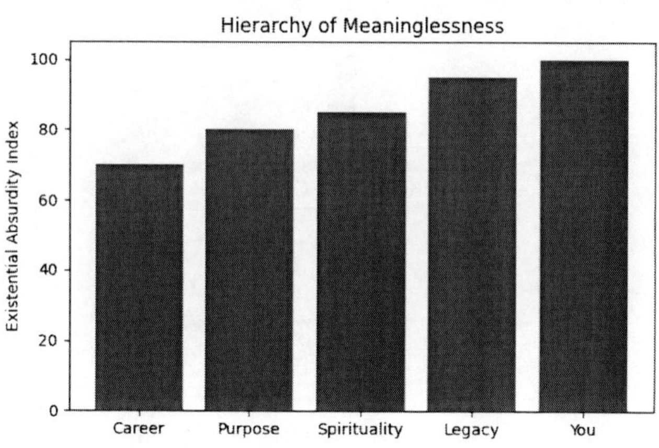

That's when I understood: the tragedy isn't that we're insignificant; it's that we're constantly auditioning for a play no one's watching. We build sandcastles and then file complaints when the waves arrive. We confuse survival with significance, and meaning with marketing. We turn even suffering into content. The gods, if they exist, must be laughing hysterically, binge-watching humanity like a cosmic sitcom with terrible writing.

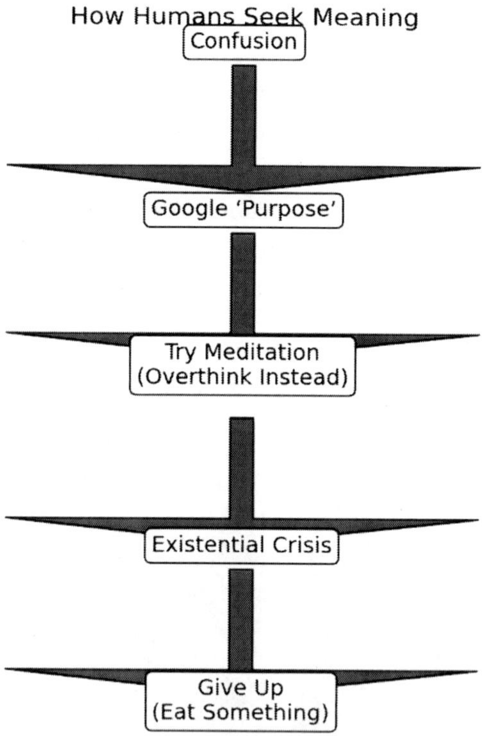

But this isn't a tragedy, it's a parody. I wasn't born for a reason. None of us was. We were born because two people got careless, drunk, or hopeful. Yet here I am, pretending the universe owes me purpose. And somehow, realising that nothing matters made everything luminous. Because once you see that the sandcastle will be washed away anyway, you can finally enjoy building it.

That's when Osho and Gibran entered the scene like old friends showing up unannounced. Osho, the Zen trickster, laughed at everything sacred; Gibran, the poetic whisperer, turned sorrow into beauty. They both taught me to dance with life rather than demand meaning from it. Osho once said, "Life in itself has no meaning. Life is an opportunity to create meaning." Gibran countered gently, "Your joy is your sorrow unmasked." Between them, I found the rhythm I'd been missing.

It hit me: life doesn't need to matter to be magnificent. The need for significance is just another addiction. I let go of the fantasy of being important, of rehearsing my obituary. I died before I died, and what remained was silence. A silence alive, deep, and strangely liberating. In that quiet, I met myself, not the self that performs, but the one that simply is. I'm not here pretending to be some guru on a hill, handing out life advice like spiritual candy. I'm not enlightened; I can barely remember my Wi-Fi password. But I do know one thing:

The only "temporary" worth having is Life.

Death is the one constant you don't have to chase. It will find you. Life? That's the slippery one. It comes, it stays for a bit, it packs up and leaves without warning. And in that tiny, inconvenient gap between "here" and "gone," you are supposed to figure out how to exist without driving yourself insane. Somewhere, a river flows, not to reach the ocean, not to impress the mountain it fell from, but simply because flowing is what it does. A tree shakes off some leaves without filing a resignation letter in triplicate. Clouds pass overhead, bloated and self-satisfied, with no idea where they're going and no quarterly targets to meet. A flower blooms in complete anonymity, aware it will die unseen, and still spends everything it has on the performance. No audience, no applause. Just blind devotion to the farce. And in this quiet madness, Life remembers something it had misplaced for millennia:

Things are happening. Everything is happening. And yet… nothing is happening.

No one is keeping score. No celestial accountant is scribbling in the Great Ledger of Meaning. No intergalactic award show is preparing to crown *"Best Performing River of 2025."*

It is all… absurdly beautiful.

Pointless. Elegant. Free.

The tragedy is never that humans are small or insignificant. The tragedy is that they keep auditioning for roles in a play no one is watching. They spend their days building sandcastles and then filing formal complaints to the waves for "vandalism." They petition the gods for meaning as if meaning were a lost AirPod. They sprint through their existence screaming, *"Look at me! I'm making an impact!"* while a blade of grass, crushed underfoot, stands back up with more dignity and far less noise.

In making everything "matter," they forget how to let anything just exist.

So Life takes a deep breath, not out of stress, but because breathing is what you do when you're alive and not choking on your own self-importance. It smiles, not a holy, glowing smile of enlightenment, but a small, almost guilty one. The kind you give when you realise the cosmic joke has been on you this whole time, and the punchline is… you.

"Maybe," Life thinks, "the point was never the point. Maybe the point was the dance. The wind. The sigh. The unspectacular sunset. The breathtaking mediocrity of being." Maybe the revolution has already happened, in the stillness, in the forgetfulness, in the sweet, sacred boredom of being alive without constantly tweeting about it.

The ants march. The wind whispers. The moon continues to not give a single damn.

Meanwhile, down on Earth, humans are still very busy trying to matter. One is giving a TED Talk titled *"Unlocking Your Inner Legacy (Before It's Too Late)."* Another is turning his trauma into content, deep-frying it for algorithmic approval. A third is angrily tweeting into the void, confident that their outrage is a form of activism.

Bless their frantic little hearts.

Up in the Great Silence, Life exhales, not out of despair, but relief. The curtain has been down for aeons, and the actors are still improvising to an empty theatre. You see, we humans have taken the idea of meaning and turned it into a full-blown addiction. We've snorted significance off the backs of sacred texts, injected it into job titles, mainlined it through romantic ideals, and still found ourselves bored on Sunday afternoons. Somewhere along the way, we confused *survival* with *significance*. And in doing so, we became terribly entertaining to the gods, who, if they exist, are most likely rolling on divine floors laughing, binge-watching humanity like a cosmic sitcom with far too many plot holes.

But don't be sad. This isn't a tragedy.

It's a parody.

The universe didn't whisper your name into the womb. It doesn't have a master plan with your face on it. And yet, here you are, looking for meaning in a place that's never heard of it. And here's the kicker:

That's beautiful.

Because once you realise life doesn't matter, you are free. Free to play, to dance, to create, to destroy, to laugh, not because it counts, but precisely because it doesn't.

A sandcastle is more exquisite because the tide is coming.

A joke is funnier when there's no punchline.

And a life lived without purpose?

That might just be the most honest life of all.

So take a breath.

Drop the script.

The performance is over.

There's no standing ovation coming. No divine Yelp review waiting to be posted. No karmic scoreboard tallying up your points. The curtain is already drawn, and the audience left ages ago. All that's left… is you.

And that absurd little spark inside you that still insists on laughing, even as the lights go out.

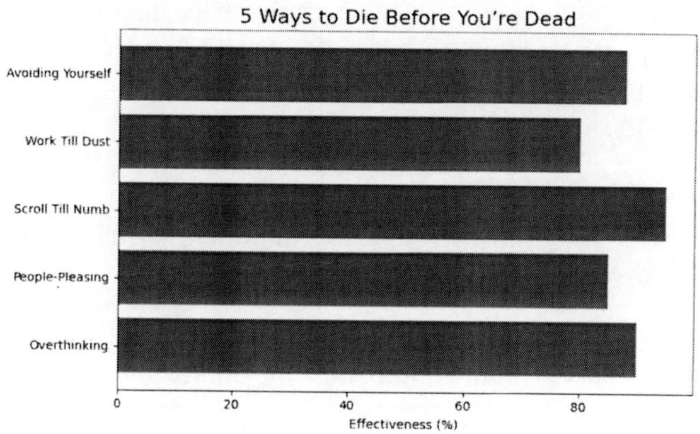

Osho and Gibran

I have been deeply inspired by the works of Osho and Khalil Gibran, for they have shown that it is possible for a human being to live with both feet firmly planted in reality while keeping the spirit open to wonder. Osho, with his razor-sharp wit and fearless dismantling of societal illusions, invites us to question everything we've been taught, not to replace one belief with another, but to step into a space where we can see life as it is. Gibran, on the other hand, moves like poetry through the human heart, weaving beauty, longing, and truth into words that speak directly to the soul.

Together, their works offer a rare balance: the pragmatism to navigate the world as it is, and the depth to remain rooted in the timeless. They remind us that spirituality is not an escape from life's chaos, but a way to dance within it without losing ourselves. I would recommend everyone, no matter their age or background, to spend time with their writing. Not to blindly follow, but to discover, perhaps for the first time, the quiet, uncompromising freedom of thinking for oneself while living in tune with something larger than the self.

Gibran, gentle as always, arrives first, not to explain life's meaninglessness, but to remind us that its beauty has never needed meaning in the first place.

"Your joy is your sorrow unmasked... The deeper that sorrow carves into your being, the more joy you can contain."

He isn't here to cheer anyone up. He's here to ruin the party by pointing out the obvious: the depth of life has nothing to do with its purpose. A rose doesn't bloom because it has a mission, it blooms because blooming is its nature. And when it withers, it doesn't file a complaint with the universe. It just dies with grace. No drama. No motivational TED talk.

Then Osho strolls in, barefoot and grinning, the Zen clown who torches the altar and then dances in the ashes like he's at a rave for nihilists.

"Life in itself has no meaning. Life is an opportunity to create meaning."

But even then, he warns against the trap. Creating meaning is like tattooing a moustache on the Mona Lisa, amusing, maybe even necessary for your own entertainment, but ultimately just a private joke. Meaning is your graffiti on the wall of Nothingness. Pretty? Sometimes. Important? Never.

Both Gibran and Osho, wildly different in tone, yet identical in essence, conspire to tell the scandalous truth:

Life doesn't need to matter to be magnificent.

And yet, here you are, dear reader, clutching at meaning like a drowning man clutching a paper straw. I get it. We've all done it. We were raised in cults called "society," handed golden chains and told they were freedom. Told to pursue jobs, reputations, love stories, and "leaving a legacy," as if we were unpaid interns in the marketing department of the cosmos.

So here's the part you're going to hate:

Let it go.

Let go of the fantasy that you need to be important. Let go of the polite little obituary you've been rehearsing in your head. Let go of the desperate need for your life to "mean" something. Die before you die, and watch what's left standing.

What's left is not a hero's journey. It's not a grand narrative.

It's not even "you" in the way you've been tricked into knowing yourself.

What's left is silence, thick, alive, and almost suspiciously comfortable. It's laughter that doesn't need a punchline. It's love, not as hunger, but as perfume. And yes, it's death, not the cloaked reaper, but the slow, almost polite dissolving of every lie you've been living. When life forgets to matter… it finally starts living. And it's both the most tragic and the funniest damn thing you'll ever see. We talk about "What you seek is seeking you." Let's understand this:

Seeker

O Wise One, I have travelled far, through mountains of suffering and rivers of regret, to find you.

Please, tell me the meaning of life.

Sought

Have you tried tea?

Seeker

What?

Sought

You look tense. Try tea. Meaning tastes better when you're slightly hydrated.

Seeker

I am not here for tea! I am here for Truth!

I've meditated for seven years, eaten kale against my will, and renounced casual sex. Surely that counts for something?

Sought

Points for effort.

Minus ten for ego.

Final score: still lost.

Seeker

But I've read scriptures! I've followed gurus! I've practised silence for 30 days!

Sought

And yet here you are… talking.

Seeker

I demand answers!

Sought

How adorable.

Do you also demand that clouds stop moving, or that time take a nap?

Seeker

You mock me.

Sought

No, I mirror you. You mock yourself, sincerely.

Seeker

Then what is the point of seeking?

Sought

To exhaust yourself. Until there's no seeker left.

And then, in the beautiful boredom that follows, you might finally notice:

You were always home.

But you insisted on knocking.

Seeker

So… there is no meaning?

Sought

Not unless you invent one. Preferably over tea.

Seeker

So then you are not the Truth?

Sought

I'm not even *real*.

I'm a hallucination born from your craving to be someone who finds something.

Seeker

Then who am I?

Sought

Ah. The only truly interesting question.

But by the time you answer it, "you" may no longer exist.

And that... would be delightful.

Seeker

I'm confused.

Sought

Good. Confusion is the first honest emotion you've had all day.

Seeker

So what should I do now?

Sought

Dance. Laugh. Make tea. Burn your old journals. Watch ants build things that will be destroyed by your careless foot.

Live like none of these matters, because it doesn't.

And that, dear Seeker… is the most sacred truth I can offer.

The Sacred Pointlessness of It All

Before you rush off to tattoo this last line onto your inner thigh, fathom this:

A child builds a sandcastle.

Not for awards.

Not for Instagram.

Not for a portfolio.

When the tide strolls in and eats it like a bored god, the kid laughs… and just builds another.

Now, picture a CEO doing the same.

He hires a consultant, conducts market research on optimal grain density, files for a sandcastle patent, and when the tide comes in, he sues the ocean.

We laugh. But it's us. We've lost the child but kept the tantrum. And the river, oh, the poor, purposeless river, just flows. Not toward success. Not toward nirvana. Just… flows.

If the river is human, it stops halfway, hires a life coach, and wonders if it's living up to its "aquatic potential." "Should I be a waterfall instead? Am I just a stream living someone else's truth?" Meanwhile, life, that messy, swirling improvisation, never once asks to be meaningful. It just is. Trees aren't in therapy about their bark-to-leaf ratio. Birds don't sit in vision-board workshops before they sing.

And death? Death is the only character in this circus who minds its business. No speeches. No big talk. No "before I go, I just want to say." Just a polite, unshakable: "Enough."

Death proves it, all our meanings are cosplay.

Achievements? Mulched.

Your grand quest for purpose? Adorable.

And still…

Inside this big, cosmic prank is a freedom so outrageous it could give you vertigo if it weren't also hilarious. The freedom to be the child again. To play for no reason. To laugh without a setup. To live without a mission statement. To die without needing to have "mattered."

To be able to create a world around you that is dangerously free, not the polite, Instagrammable freedom that comes with yoga mats and overpriced herbal tea, but the kind of freedom that unsettles people. A freedom that laughs at rules, pokes holes in grand life plans, and rejoices in its own absurdity like a drunk jester in a court of kings who take themselves far too seriously.

The whole idea of "achieving something" should feel so utterly pointless that it collapses under its own weight, leaving you with nothing but a lightness that no motivational guru can sell. Then, my dear readers, you might find yourself asking, *"Why the hell should we live? Are you leading us straight into the dark alley of meaninglessness? Do you think life is not worth living? Are you secretly depressed? You really should see a therapist."*

To which I say, with all the warmth of a rattlesnake in winter, *I don't give a damn.* Your need for meaning is your addiction, not my problem. My only point, and it's a point worth tattooing on your forehead if you have the courage, is to give you a bird's-eye view of life from death's point of view.

Why not walk backwards from death into life? Imagine starting at the end: the body cold, the breath gone, the story over. From there, each step you take "backwards" is a bonus, a ridiculous gift. Suddenly, the traffic jam doesn't seem so bad, the unpaid bills are just paper, and the heartbreak you thought would kill you feels more like bad theatre.

It's interesting, isn't it? If you truly saw the finish line first, you might stop sprinting like a maniac to get somewhere. You might stroll. You might sit down. You might even laugh, because you'd finally see that the whole thing is a cosmic prank, and the only winning move is to enjoy losing beautifully.

Here's the cosmic punchline: even those relationships, those sacred bonds forged in fluorescent offices over coffee and invoices, will be forgotten eventually. Your supplier's grandson will not care how loyally you paid on time. Your customer's great-granddaughter will not remember that you once gave a discount that saved her grandmother's wedding. And your own lineage, if you're lucky enough to have one, will recall you fondly for maybe two generations before filing you away in the great archive of irrelevance. By the time your third generation is fully grown, your name is a trivia question, your face a sepia-toned blur on a shelf no one dusts.

This is where the mythology of "legacy" collapses. Humans build statues so pigeons have toilets. They write books so future generations can underline the same clichés with fresh pens. They endow scholarships so their name can be mispronounced at graduation ceremonies long after they're gone. Legacy is simply our desperate attempt to graffiti our names on the bathroom wall of time, hoping eternity doesn't repaint. Spoiler: it always does.

So why bother? Why suffocate yourself trying to be remembered by people who won't even remember to charge their phones? You don't need to create a legacy.

You need to create a moment. A blissful state of being, even if it lasts as briefly as the fizz of soda in a warm glass. Sit with your tea. Laugh at your own absurdity. Love someone without the HR paperwork of reciprocity. Live as if the whole game is a rehearsal, not a performance. Because it is.

If you must leave something behind, let it be laughter echoing in someone's kitchen, or silence that made someone comfortable, or the simple memory that you didn't take yourself too seriously. These can't be carved into stone or passed down through three generations, but they don't need to be. They are their own reward.

But we humans are terrible at sitting with the truth. Silence scares us; freedom feels like loneliness; so, we built an escape route and called it God. A celestial complaint department for everything we can't explain, a cosmic HR head to file grievances with when life doesn't go as planned. We've outsourced both accountability and wonder to a being we barely understand. And in doing so, we've turned mystery into mythology and fear into faith. We invented Him to comfort our fears and ended up using Him to justify them. Every temple became a negotiation table, every prayer a demand letter. Somewhere along the way, God stopped being a mystery and became a mascot.

And if anyone has truly suffered in the hands of man, it's not man, it's God.

Chapter - 2

I Am God (Identifies as He/Him)

I have been reduced to a mere wish-fulfiller. It's less worship, more transaction. A cosmic barter system. Humans show up with incense sticks, flowers, garlands, quilts, even leaves, as if I, the supposed creator of galaxies, am in urgent need of home décor and aromatherapy. And when that's not enough, they toss in money. As though bribing me like some underpaid bureaucrat at the RTO would get them their learning license.

And I sit there, in whichever franchise they've parked me in, temple, church, mosque, take your pick, wondering: *Really? I created humans for this circus? For an endless chorus of "gimme, gimme, gimme"?*

Where's the gratitude? Where's the care? Not once has anyone asked me, "Hey God, eaten yet? Had a decent nap?" Apparently, omnipotence comes with zero self-care checks. And the cruel joke? If they actually saw me, they'd probably kill me. Oh wait! Haven't they done that already, multiple times over? Yes. Many, many times.

So here I am, reduced to a celestial moron, blessing them for literally nothing. Maybe the wisest move is to disappear altogether. Log out. Vanish. Never return to this Godforsaken planet. And here's the kicker!! Most God Franchisees assume I'm male. Bearded, booming, with suspiciously muscular calves under the holy robe. But what if I wasn't? What if I were a woman? Ah, then the whole game changes. Because if I turned out to be a woman, every offering of money, flowers, and incense would suddenly look like cheap pickup lines at a cosmic bar. Men would panic, egos would collapse, and religions would have to rewrite their entire PR campaign. Blasphemy, indeed.

Am I a Woman?

If I were a Woman, history would read like a crime confession. Every cathedral, mosque, and temple would have to issue an apology, every scripture would have to be pulped, and every man in a position of divine authority would have to admit that he'd been mansplaining the cosmos to its rightful owner.

The very question *Am I a Woman?* Is an insult disguised as curiosity. As if you're asking whether the sun could, in theory, rise in the west. You have built an entire architecture of belief on the assumption that I have a beard, a deep voice, and a patriarchal fondness for male heirs. Why? Because if I were a woman, your entire power pyramid would collapse into a sad little pile of male insecurity and unpaid emotional labour.

If I were a woman, the Ten Commandments would've been fifteen, and five of them would simply read

1. Pick up your socks.
2. Call your mother.
3. Listen, don't fix.
4. No, I'm not mad, I'm *disappointed.*
5. Wash the dishes before the locust plague starts.

If I were a Woman, there would be no "mysterious ways." There'd be calendars, spreadsheets, and reminders: "You had six thousand years to stop killing each other. Now, hand over the matches." There'd be no holy wars, only silent treatment so profound that nations would collapse under the weight of it.

And maybe that's why you invented Male God. You needed someone who wouldn't notice the mess until it was on fire. A God who could be bribed with smoke and flowers, who'd "let boys be boys" while genocides happened off-camera. A God who wouldn't mind being invoked to bless wars, tax fraud, and football games. If I were a Woman, I'd remember *everything*. Every broken promise, every whispered prayer, every time you said "I'll change" and didn't. You wouldn't need hell; your own guilt would chew you alive. And so, you kept me hypothetical. You wrote me out of the story. You called me blasphemy before I could call you accountability. Because deep down, you knew the truth: if I were a Woman, the Judgment Day wouldn't be a trial, it'd be an intervention.

The truth is, we men have always been terrified of the possibility that God could show up as a woman. If She descended from the clouds in all Her glory, the entire male power structure would collapse overnight. The centuries-old façade would crumble, the priesthood would faint, and our fragile egos would be flattened like plastic bottles in a power press. Imagine the horror: a God who menstruates, multitasks, and remembers every single lie you've ever told. A God you'd have to ask for directions. A God who'd say, "No, you can't bomb that country! Now go clean your room." Better to keep the beard, the deep voice, and the sky-throne than to risk Her showing up and saying, "Alright, boys, hand me the steering wheel, you've clearly made a mess of things."

But instead, God has been the most misunderstood celestial being of all, and that's saying something, because humans misunderstand *everything.* We have reduced the infinite to a kind of supernatural shopkeeper, an overworked, underpaid genie who exists solely to grant our petty wishes. "Dear God, give me a promotion." "Dear God, make my child pass mathematics." "Dear God, let my neighbour's car mysteriously break down." We treat the divine as though it's an eternal customer service line, with prayer as the hold music and temple donations as our transaction fee.

I am a Hindu, so I know the drill. We march into the temple like customers queuing at a help desk, coconut in one hand, flowers in the other, milk sloshing around in a dented pot, ready to initiate a sacred transaction. "Here you go, God! premium offerings, freshly purchased from that overpriced shop outside. Now, in return, please fix my job, my marriage, my acne, and my child's exam results." It's as if God is some celestial cashier who trades blessings for biodegradable items. And the irony? None of these offerings is even remotely usable. Coconut water? Spilt on the floor. Flowers? Dead within hours. Milk? Poured over a stone idol until it curdles into temple cheese. And the incense? Oh yes, nothing says "divine connection" like forcing your deity to inhale a blend of carbon monoxide, ash, and cheap sandalwood perfume until His cosmic lungs wheeze. Honestly, if God is omniscient, He probably knows exactly when the crowd is coming and schedules a nap. Imagine being all-powerful and still having to endure a daily fog of smoke, muttered requests for promotions, and a line of people waving bananas in your face. If I were her, I'd fake poor network connectivity: *"Sorry, your prayer could not be delivered at this time. Please try again after enlightenment."*

But tell me, dear reader: is your God so impoverished that He awaits your offerings like a beggar at the temple gate? Does she sit there, shivering in eternity, waiting for you to cover her with a quilt stitched from your superstition? Is the Creator of galaxies parched for the few spoonfuls of milk you pour on stone, as if the nectar of existence itself could curdle without your dairy? Is the Almighty, who spins universes on the tip of a fingernail, stranded in a tropical drought, praying for your coconut to save Him from thirst? The thought would be comic if it weren't so tragic. And yet we persist, with folded hands and furrowed brows, as if the rhythm of the cosmos hinges not on stars collapsing into black holes, but on whether we remembered to buy the right marigolds from the market. And perhaps the cruellest truth is this: if God *is* watching, maybe the coconuts and flowers are not tokens of love, but proof that we have absolutely no idea who or what we're dealing with. Maybe we don't worship God at all. Maybe we worship the idea that the universe should revolve around us, and in that case, the idol we bow before isn't divine, it's our own bloated reflection.

And for this very reason, God has been out of work for a while now.

Sure, He still gets tagged in every conceivable crisis, blamed for tsunamis, praised for football goals, quoted by politicians who use Him like a prop in a bad play. But behind the scenes, His desk is empty. His inbox: rotting with unread prayers. His calendar: one long lunch break with Eternity, the kind where the waiter never brings the bill because the meal never ends.

But we like the transaction. It keeps the illusion alive: I give You flowers, You give me miracles. And when the miracles don't come, we call it "God's mysterious ways" instead of what it really is, silence. If there *is* a God, and that's the most generous 'if' you'll hear from me, then He is not the benevolent grandfather we've painted. He's a playwright who gets bored halfway through the story, a joker of a circus trying to tell you a joke seriously, or at max a friend who tells you when you have been an asshole (some call it your conscience, others call it gut feeling). We all know, we all have defied our own intuitions, our own subconscious, but never admitted to it. We all know we are killing in the name of God, burning effigies in His name and raping women because she is a witch (she was just offering a prayer in a way that the world doesn't subscribe to). Either this is the most elaborate divine joke ever told, or the Author has walked away from the typewriter entirely, leaving us all to rot in a half-finished script.

In the Beginning, Man Created God

Man created God, of course, not out of faith, but out of fear. Fear of lightning, fear of death, fear of women who speak their mind without asking for male approval first. God was basically our celestial insurance policy: *"Obey the invisible man and no bad thing shall befall you"* unless, of course, He was in a bad mood, in which case you could expect plagues, floods, or relatives visiting unannounced. He was the original Terms & Conditions nobody read, but somehow everyone was legally bound by. And for a while, it worked. God had *fantastic* PR. Priests, Pundits, Maulvis, the original marketing team rallied behind Him. They became the middlemen of eternity, running a divine customer service desk: *"Press 1 for forgiveness, Press 2 for rain, Press 3 to smite your enemies."* Naturally, this service came with a small processing fee, usually in cash, gold, women or your eternal obedience. Their job was to keep the fear alive, the miracle alive, and the charm alive. And what a job they did! Sales skyrocketed. Then they scaled. Took it global. Now everyone is scared of God, atheists included ("What if there's a divine force?"). Even God Himself probably wakes up at 3 a.m. sometimes thinking, *"What have I done? My little Frankensteins are wreaking havoc all around the world. This is not what I signed up for."* The irony is delicious: the all-powerful Creator, now a hostage of His own fan club.

Omnipotent!!!! Omniscient!!!!! Omnipresent!!!!!

But with very human scheduling issues, rarely available during genocides, oddly responsive to sports prayers. We gave Him robes, a beard, a booming voice, and naturally, a penis. (Omnipotence, apparently, wasn't enough. He needed external genitalia to assert dominance. He became the all-powerful sky-father with surprisingly human insecurities.

Jealous. Angry. Easily offended.

Basically, the CEO of a morally questionable startup called Existence™, where unpaid interns were expected to worship the management 24/7 and still be grateful for the opportunity. When people asked hard questions: *Why suffering? Why evil? Why mosquitoes?*

His earthly representatives leaned in and said,

"It's a mystery."

Which, in religious terms, translates to

"Shut up and tithe."

But then, tragedy struck. Humans learned to read. We started asking better questions. We split the atom, built space telescopes, cured smallpox, and yes, invented flavoured water that glows in the dark. Suddenly, "God did it" didn't pass peer review. Creation myths collapsed under carbon dating. Hell lost its sting once air conditioning was invented. Heaven? Still a solid concept, but the entry criteria remained suspiciously vague, like the dress code at an elite nightclub run by angels with clipboards. And so, the God of Commandments and Consequences…was downsized.

Like a retired rock star still doing greatest hits in half-empty churches, surrounded by die-hard fans and a smell of incense that can't quite mask the mildew of irrelevance.

We didn't kill God.

We ghosted Him.

Today, He lingers like an outdated operating system. Still running in the background of anxious minds. Still invoked during plane turbulence, last-stage cancer, and election campaigns.

But mostly, we've moved on.

Now we worship the algorithm. Pray to Wi-Fi. Confess on social media. Find salvation in dopamine loops and discount codes. We replaced the pulpit with the podcast. The sacrament with supplements. The divine with the curated. God 2.0 has no beard, but excellent branding.

He doesn't judge; he just personalises your feed.

And ironically, this version is harder to escape. Because, unlike the old God, who at least took Sundays off, this one follows you everywhere. In your pocket. In your thoughts. In your carefully staged breakfast photos. But here's the real punchline:

Even with all our progress, our tech, our data...

We're still terrified. Of death. Of silence. Of meaninglessness. Which is why we keep clinging to God. We want to keep living, we want to be rich, and we want all the pleasures of the world. What we forget in the process is that Godliness is a dimension that has been forgotten by many.

We still somehow believe in God but have completely ghosted Godliness, like that friend you used to hang out with because they had a Netflix account. Godliness, in my definition, is the entire existence bowing with you in gratitude to this wonderful phenomenon called life, with no hashtags and no spiritual influencers making reels about it. It's smiling back at a child without checking if they have sticky hands, not bargaining with street vendors (yes, you who paid ₹800 for a cocktail that was 90% ice, no cock, no tail, just frozen water with an identity crisis), sitting with elderly people without checking your phone every thirty seconds, or visiting a holy place just to bow in gratitude rather than to update your WhatsApp status.

He provides for your lusts, your addictions, your shallow ambitions, and in return, He gets *nothing*.

What kind of diseased relationship is this, where one side gives endlessly, and the other only takes?

If this were between humans, we'd call it abuse.

Between you and God, we call it "faith."

Animals don't bother with this hypocrisy. They don't worship, they don't kneel, they don't moralise. They live the day, they survive, they sleep, they rise. No sanctimony. No bargaining. No false humility.

Just existence, pure, unflinching, unadorned. And maybe that's why they seem more divine than us: because they never had to invent a God to excuse their cruelty, or a religion to disguise their greed

Now go.

Bake a cake.

Take a nap.

Water a plant without asking it for a sign from the universe.

God won't mind.

He's retired.

Let's clear something up, once and for all.

God, the one with the beard, the throne, the emotional issues, is a myth. A middle manager invented by early humans who couldn't handle thunderstorms or women menstruating in peace.

Godliness, on the other hand, is real. Terrifyingly, magnificently, quietly real.

God is someone you argue over.

Godliness is something you shut up for.

God is quoted by angry people on TV.

Godliness lives in a dog licking your face after eating something unspeakable.

God divides temples, churches, and egos.

Godliness grows silently in the cracks of forgotten sidewalks.

God demands worship.

Godliness doesn't even notice you exist.

You can't institutionalise Godliness. There's no entry fee, no priest, no subscription model.

It doesn't care if you're vegan, enlightened, or have 108 crystals in your bathroom.

Godliness shows up in the way a leaf falls, perfectly, pointlessly.

In the way a child laughs at dust.

In the way death erases a name without malice.

Godliness is not *in* things.

It *is* things.

The bark of a mangy street dog.

The curve of a broken teacup.

The silence after someone says, "I love you," and means it.

So next time you feel the urge to bow, don't do it in a building named after an invisible boss.

Bow to the wind.

Bow to the rotting banana on your kitchen counter.

Bow to the absurdity of your own heartbeat.

Bow to the fact that none of this has to make sense, and yet it still *moves.*

Because Godliness has no face, no name, no message.

It just is.

Like a joke the universe told itself, and then forgot the punchline.

A Brief Interview with God

Interviewer: God, thank You for joining us. First question: What is the meaning of life?

God: *Why does everyone assume I wrote the script? I was just hired to do lighting.*

Interviewer: What about suffering?

God: *Well, you invented money, marriage, and organised religion. I just watched.*

Interviewer: Are you… real?

God: *Does it matter? You're all doing improv theatre with full commitment.*

Interviewer: What would you say to humanity?

God: *Loosen up. Stop praying for parking spaces. Eat fruit. Forgive your father. And maybe, just maybe, try not taking yourselves so seriously. It's unbecoming. Look for Godliness instead*

Interviewer: Wait, what?

A Prayer to That Which Never Asked for One

O nameless, formless, delightfully disinterested presence, you who reside equally in cat vomit and cathedral light, accept this offering of nothing.

We bow not to You but to the fact that You don't care if we bow.

We praise You, not for miracles or morality, but for continuing to let humans exist despite their group chats and YouTube comments.

You, who speak not in scripture but in the awkward silence between two strangers on a bus.

You, who move not through thunder or revelation, but through the way sunlight hits a pile of trash and makes it look, for one brief second, like art.

You who hide inside dog piss on a holy wall, inside a dying grandmother's last joke, inside the breath of a man who thinks he's finally figured it all out, only to stub his toe on enlightenment's coffee table.

Bless us with more confusion.

More laughter that makes the stomach hurt.

More moments that strip us naked of purpose and leave us standing there, blinking… free.

Deliver us from the need to matter.

Lead us not into ambition, but into the temptation of stillness.

For Yours is the nowhere, the nonsense, and the now.

Forever and ever,

ha.

God's CV: As Submitted to the Universe

Name: God (mononyms are cool)

Date of Birth: Timeless (don't ask)

Current Address: Classified (mail forwarding not available.)

Objective:

To maintain omnipotence without having to actually deal with people.

To sustain the illusion of involvement while quietly outsourcing miracles to chance. Creating an illusion of mysteriousness while playing poker with Demi Gods.

Work Experience

- **Creation, Universe Inc. (∞ - present)**
  - Invented light, darkness, and a suspiciously specific number of dimensions.
  - Designed humans with opposable thumbs and a self-destruct button called "ego."
  - Accidentally created mosquitoes, pretended it was on purpose.
  - Implemented "free will" as a beta feature, never debugged.
  - Designed trees as life givers, watches humans cut them down for toilet rolls.

Miracle Production (Freelance)

- **Created Universe** - Mostly for the aesthetic. Still debated endlessly by atheists and theists, both of whom sound equally exhausting at dinner parties.

- **Water into wine -** Still a bestseller among alcoholics, desperate wedding hosts, and church fundraisers. Miracles sold separately, hangover not included.
- **Parted a sea -** Got one-star Yelp reviews from Pharaoh: *"Would not recommend. Lost half my workforce. Overpriced. Smelled like fish."*
- **Provided manna from heaven -** Cancelled after too many complaints about gluten, carbs, and lack of vegan options.
- **Killed evil people like Ravana -** But also told his wife to *literally* sit on a fire pit to prove her innocence, because apparently marriage counselling wasn't invented yet.
- **Drank poison for the world's good -** Also chopped off his son's head in a fit of cosmic drama, then replaced it with an elephant head. The son was surprisingly okay with it, proving kids in mythology had better adaptability than modern toddlers with Wi-Fi.

Key Skills

- Passive-aggressive omnipresence.
- Cryptic communication via burning foliage or sending OM into the space for humans to figure out.
- Smite-on-demand (terms and conditions apply).

- Selective compassion, usually based on plot twist requirements.
- Occasional t sunamis, floods and earthquakes.
- Will show face if worshipped for 500 years.

Notable Achievements

- Maintained top deity status despite zero rebranding in 2000 years.
- Outsmarted philosophers by never showing up for interviews.
- Delegated moral law to humans, watched them turn it into a tax system.

References

- Abraham (contact info lost)
- Vishnu (Theatre personality)
- Moses (burning bush enthusiast)
- Oprah (long story)

But God's been out of the office for a while now. Here's where He's been spotted since His last major miracle:

1. Backpacking in Andromeda

Wearing flip-flops and a galaxy-print hoodie, sipping cosmic lattes while ignoring prayers like unopened spam. Occasionally tells locals, "Yeah, I used to run Earth," only to get polite nods.

2. Running a Taco Stand in Dimension 9

Speciality: fish tacos that actually *multiply* if you leave them alone. Menu slogan: *"Come for the salsa, stay because time is an illusion."*

3. Weekly Poker Nights with Buddha, Nietzsche, and Two Sentient Clouds

Buddha folds every hand ("non-attachment"), Nietzsche cheats ("God is dead, but I'm not"), and the clouds just weep softly when they lose. God usually wins, but insists it's "divine luck."

4. Watching Humans from a Safe Distance

Like an ex stalking your Instagram stories, God still checks in sometimes, just to see what you're ruining now. He laughs when billionaires thank Him for their yachts, then cries when the same people ignore starving kids in His name.

5. Writing a Memoir He'll Never Publish

Tentative title: *It's Not Me, It's You: A Creator's Guide to Walking Away.* Currently, 900 pages of notes, mostly "Why did I even bother?"

But we continue to be the little cry- babies that we are. Still howling, still complaining. No reasoning, no rationale, no literature review. Just pure unadulterated belief that He will do the needful. No, Sir, He/she will not. Your consciousness, on the other hand, might do the trick. Uplift yourself into the realms of deep thinking, travelling inwards, and you might find the answer.

The Holy Complaint Department

*(**Established:** Day 6 of Creation. Staffed: Nobody. Response time: Eternity.)*

Ancient Era Complaints (Pre-Wi-Fi Prayer Requests)

1. **Complaint:** "Dear God, the crops failed again. Do you even read these? Or do I need to sacrifice a bigger goat?"

   God's Auto-Reply: *"Bigger goat. Always bigger goat. Think bigger."*

2. **Complaint:** *"Dear God, thanks for inventing women. But... why childbirth?"*

   God's Auto-Reply: *"Because watching grown men faint in delivery rooms is my favourite reality show."*

3. **Complaint:** *"Dear God, I prayed for rain. You sent a flood. Overachiever much?"*

   God's Auto-Reply: *"You're welcome."*

4. **Complaint:** *"Dear God, why give snakes the ability to talk if all they're gonna do is ruin fruit for everyone?"*

   God's Auto-Reply: *"Content creation. Every story needs a villain."*

5. **Complaint:** *"Dear God, I brought two pigeons and a sack of grain as an offering. The neighbour brought a full ox. Please smite him for showing off."*

God's Auto-Reply: *"Noted. Will promote him to village chief."*

Medieval Complaints (When Faith Came with a Side of Plague)

1. **Complaint:** *"Dear God, can you explain why the Black Death happened to us but not to the rich merchant's family who cheats on weights? Asking for a continent."*

   God's Auto-Reply: *"Because his wife makes great pies."*

2. **Complaint:** *"Dear God, I joined the Crusades because you said it was holy. Why am I dying of dysentery in a desert?"*

   God's Auto-Reply: *"Fine print. You should have read the fine print."*

3. **Complaint:** *"Dear God, thanks for the feudal system. Love working for scraps while the bishop rides a horse made of gold."*

   God's Auto-Reply: *"Gold horse? Nice. I might get one too."*

4. **Complaint:** *"Dear God, if the Earth is flat like the priests say, why do my ships keep falling off the edge into Portugal?"*

   God's Auto-Reply: *"Because you're drunk, Harold."*

5. **Complaint:** *"Dear God, I have fasted for forty days. Now I'm dead. Was that the goal?"*

God's Auto-Reply: *"Yes."*

Modern Complaints (Now with Hashtags)

1. **Complaint:** *"Dear God, my Wi-Fi went down in the middle of my Netflix binge. Why do you test me so?"*

   God's Auto-Reply: *"Because you still haven't watched that documentary about climate change."*

2. **Complaint:** *"Dear God, my Uber driver took a wrong turn, and now I'm late to yoga. This is literally the worst thing to happen in history."*

   God's Auto-Reply: *"Tell that to Pompeii."*

3. **Complaint:** *"Dear God, thanks for the mangoes, but why the pit? Was that really necessary?"*

   God's Auto-Reply: *"Because I like to watch you work for it."*

4. **Complaint:** *"Dear God, if you could stop making mosquitoes, that would be great. Nobody's out here praying for them."*

   God's Auto-Reply: *"You're not supposed to like all my creations. Keeps you humble."*

5. **Complaint:** *"Dear God, I manifested a millionaire boyfriend. You sent me a man with crypto debt."*

   God's Auto-Reply: *"Close enough.*

What I gather from reading about different eras is that the problems changed, but God didn't, same old boss, different employee complaints. He's still stuck in the eternal soap opera of a housewife praying for a boy child ("Girl? Delete. Especially in my country"), a husband praying his neighbour would finally invite him over for tea (and maybe more), a farmer begging for rain, a warehouse owner begging for *no* rain, and of course, a writer praying his book sells millions, preferably without having to read it himself.

God sells. Godliness saves

God's plea

Subject: "It's not you, it's… actually, it is you."

Dear Humanity,

We need to talk.

This… whatever we have, isn't working.

First of all, stop using my name in your wars. I don't care if you're defending holy land, holy cows, or holy hashtags; you're embarrassing us both.

Second, stop forwarding those chain prayers. I'm God, not a desperate YouTuber begging for likes. Your "Forward this to 10 people for blessings" stunt? I don't work on referral programs.

Third, while we're here, stop pretending your petty desires are my grand plan. I didn't "bless you" with a parking spot; you just got lucky because someone left.

Fourth, please stop sending me requests for wealth, beauty, and revenge. I'm not your genie. I don't do express delivery. I *especially* don't do "manifesting."

Look, I tried to be patient. I even gave you mangoes. But you complained about the pit.

So here's the deal: I'll keep running the sun, the moon, and the laws of physics. You work on not being so… *you.*

Yours (for now),

God

Formerly Your Biggest Fan.

And if you're still confused, still wondering how to deal with me, don't worry. Humanity loves instruction manuals, so here's one last mercy:

How to Worship Godliness: The Official Fake Guide

Step 1: Shut up.

Seriously. Silence. No chants, no incense, no holy playlists. Just… shut up.

Step 2: Look at anything alive for 30 seconds.

A tree. A stray dog. A pigeon with half a beak. Your grandmother's hands.

Step 3: Forget what you saw.

No selfies, no posting it online, no telling people "I just had a profound moment." If you can remember it, you're already ruining it.

Step 4: Give something without the receipt of your virtue.

No posting "Helping the needy today", the moment you brag, you've killed it.

Step 5: Let someone else be right.

Even if they're wrong. Especially if they're wrong.

Step 6: Repeat until dead.

Congratulations. You've achieved Godliness. No certificate provided.

And that, my friends, is the art of dying.....dying with gratitude, dying with Godliness. What you search outside is hidden inside your colon (get a colonoscopy, you will find out), or maybe gut, or maybe liver, who cares. It's somewhere inside you...find out, and you will uncover things about yourself and life and death that you will not need God in its current form. Instead, you will simply be a happy person, content with life, content with death. You will not glorify your religion and mock others, you will not kill in the name of God, you will not be able to see suffering irrespective of gender, caste or creed. Then, you would have unlocked the actual meaning of life and, in the process, death. To live without clinging, and to die without begging. To be grateful for both. That is the art of dying.

And yet, right when you begin to touch that rare peace, the world interrupts, ready with a new checklist. Because peace doesn't sell, identity does. The moment you stop chasing, society hands you a fresh chase: *Become someone.*

Chapter - 3

The Myth of Becoming (Terms & Conditions Apply)

From the moment you're born: screaming, clueless, the world begins whispering in your ear:

"Become someone."

Not just anyone. No, no. Someone *special.* Someone successful, sexy, enlightened, employable, gluten-free, emotionally available but also mysteriously aloof. A curated soul with a six-figure income and a six-pack that doesn't drink six beers a night. Someone who will be the guiding light to millions. You are told, sold, and eventually made to believe this golden lie:

That *you*, in your raw, ridiculous, natural state, are not enough. And so begins the lifelong theatre of *Becoming.* Now you are in an endless trap of proving yourself to the world, your "loved" ones, now you want likes, you seek validation, accolades make you happy, praises make you feel important, make you feel you have "arrived." Where in fact, there is nothing to arrive at. The only thing worth arriving at is the conscious awareness that to be yourself in this circus of “Be Somebody” is the biggest arrival of all.

Becoming Is the Best Distraction from Being

You start small. Maybe with a fake smile at school, or pretending you liked that TED Talk. Later, you buy things. Shoes that hurt your feet but impress the tribe. Books you never finish (I doubt you will finish this one as well). Courses with the word “Mastery” in them (also books starting from “The art of”). You build an identity, brick by insecure brick, and call it "growth."

But deep down, you suspect the truth.

You’re not becoming someone. You’re becoming a better liar. A more refined version of the very nonsense you were born without.

Your original face?

Forgotten.

Buried under affirmations and resumes and online bios written in the third person:

“An accomplished visionary with a passion for disrupting paradigms.”

(**Translation:** Confused mammal, fluent in buzzwords.)

Where is the authentic, unfiltered version of you hiding? The one that doesn’t rehearse every sentence in their head before saying it, the one that laughs so hard the neighbours start wondering if you’ve finally lost it. When was the last time you laughed from your stomach? not the polite office chuckle, not the emoji-laden “LOL,” but the real, messy, undignified roar? (Chances are, it was on a Friday night when you were drunk, pissed, and calling your boss things that would get you excommunicated from HR manuals forever.)

Here's the uncomfortable truth: all these expectations, judgments, and "benchmarks of success" belong to the world, not to you. They're invoices the world keeps sending for problems you never ordered. Why pay the bill? What does it have to do with you? If you must commit to something, commit to curiosity. Read things that spark a fire in your head, dive into ideas that make you lose track of time, pursue the ridiculous, the profound, the trivial, whatever floats your boat. And read so deeply, so obsessively, that mastery sneaks up on you like a thief in the night. Not the kind of "mastery" that comes laminated in a degree you barely remember studying for, but the kind that comes from living, from following your fascinations until they become second nature.

Because here's the irony: the world worships "degrees," but it quietly bows to obsession. A mugged-up certificate may get you a cubicle; obsession gets you freedom. One makes you an employee. The other might make you an employer.

Why to become an entrepreneur

Because no one else is coming to save you.

Because the system you're told to trust runs on obedience, not originality. Because the world is already overflowing with people who wake up every day to build someone else's dream.

Entrepreneurship isn't about making money; it's about reclaiming authorship over your own life. It's a declaration that your curiosities, your experiments, your so-called "crazy ideas" deserve a chance to breathe outside PowerPoint slides and polite coffee shop conversations. It's about stepping out of the neatly labelled queue called *stability* and walking into the chaos where real creation happens.

To become an entrepreneur is to say, "I refuse to be a spectator." It's to test your courage against uncertainty, to dance with risk without needing a safety net. It's realising that passion without execution is just daydreaming, and execution without passion is wage labour. You need both, and entrepreneurship forces you to confront both every single day.

And no, you don't need venture capital or a pitch deck that could seduce Silicon Valley. You don't need fancy words like "scale," "pivot," or "exit strategy." You can start with something absurdly small. A kiosk selling tea. A stall printing t-shirts. A food cart serving three items that taste like nostalgia.

Do you know what's common between a multinational and a street vendor? Both are entrepreneurs; the difference is just the number of zeros. Even a small kiosk, run with curiosity and commitment, can create millions, not just in money, but in stories, in freedom, in the quiet satisfaction of saying, "I built this."

Entrepreneurship is the art of turning fascination into a livelihood. It's a spiritual act disguised as commerce, a form of rebellion where your imagination writes the business plan. And once you taste that freedom, you can never go back to clocking in and out for someone else's spreadsheet.

Because when you create something of your own, no matter how small, you stop being part of the machinery. You become the person who builds it. More on that later when I debunk the myths of entrepreneurship in a separate chapter (after all, I am but a professor). Now getting back to self-loathing (sorry, self-improvement)

Self-Improvement: The Classiest Form of Self-Hate

Look closely, dear reader. Self-improvement is capitalism in a kimono. It sells you back the worth you were born with, but with better fonts and a payment plan.

"Be more mindful," they say,

But only after selling you the $399 silent retreat.

"Become your best self," they chant,

As if your current self were some embarrassing software version from the Dark Ages.

You meditate, but only to forget about the monkeys dancing in your head.

You fast, but only to become more desirable.

You love, but only to feel less lonely.

It's always a transaction.

Even your pain becomes performative

"Look how broken I am. Look how deep. Please swipe right."

But let me tell you a secret

No one becomes.

They just pretend better. You wear so many masks, you forget which one eats breakfast. You become spiritual, but only after branding your trauma. You become philosophical, but only until it's time to pay taxes.

Eventually, you exhaust yourself, burn out, break down, go bald, or worse:

Become a motivational speaker.

But just before the final collapse,

There's a crack in the theatre lights,

A flicker in the script.

You realize

The one thing scarier than not becoming anyone… is realising you did not need to. You were quite the darling in your childhood, but then you lost your innocence (right time to go listen to "Return to Innocence" by Enigma).

Exit the Factory

What happens if you stop?

Not dramatically, no big declarations. Just quietly stop pretending you're on your way to a more "valid" version of yourself. You might become less impressive at parties. You might laugh more. Cry more. Get bored. Finally feel.

You might become invisible to the world, but visible to whatever godless wonder whispers in the wind through broken windows.

And that… is freedom.

Not the freedom to become.

But the freedom to become no one, and still feel alive.

The Tragedy of Trying to Be Someone You're Not (But with a Vision Board)

We live in an age where "authenticity" is a brand, where people post candid selfies after spending 45 minutes choosing the right *"I woke up like this"* filter.

Everyone's busy being "themselves," except they're doing it based on what an influencer named Luna Starblood posted on a Tuesday on Instagram.

We're told to "find ourselves" but only after losing ourselves in market trends, career hacks, and ten-step personality tests designed by ex-cult members. Here's the cosmic joke:

You never needed to find yourself.

You just needed to stop auditioning for roles you were never cast in.

Try this for one day

Be someone else. Go full method.

Talk like Deepak Chopra, dress like Steve Jobs, eat like Gwyneth Paltrow.

By noon, you'll either need a nap or a therapist. Because being someone you're not is a full-time job, with zero holidays, no pension, and a dress code that changes daily. And even when you nail it, you get applause from an audience that doesn't know your real name.

You impress everyone, except yourself.

You inspire everyone, except the child inside you who once found joy in licking walls.

Becoming a "Better Version" of Yourself: Who Approved This Idea?

Ah, yes, the Holy Grail

"I'm just working on becoming a better version of myself."

Sounds noble, right?

But have you met this "better" version?

Usually, it's just a socially acceptable hallucination:

Someone who wakes up at 5 AM, journals gratitude, microdoses ambition, smiles through burnout, and has opinions about oat milk.

But here's the thing

You can't become a "better" version of yourself by hating who you are now. That's like trying to grow a flower by yelling at the seed. Self-hate in a nice outfit is still self-hate. Improvement that comes from fear is just spiritual gentrification.

Yes, you might need to heal, grow, unlearn, and deconstruct, but not so you can become more palatable to LinkedIn.

Do it because there's an ancient intelligence in you, the same one that made trees grow and cats ignore humans, that already knows how to live. Eat right, play and do not think about things you cannot control.

Eating right is very important. And by that, I don't mean you must become a vegan monk grazing on leaves, or a hardcore non-vegetarian who believes chicken is a personality trait. What I mean is embarrassingly simple: watch how much you're eating. Not for moral reasons. For survival.

Eat mindfully. Your body will actually tell you what it wants (it's true, Google it).

And yes, eat fibre.

Fibre doesn't get enough credit in our philosophical discussions, but it should. Forget Nietzsche's abyss. The real abyss is chronic constipation.

Fruits. Vegetables. Things that have lived a life before reaching your plate.

Not things that have sat in plastic for seven months waiting for your self-destruction.

The golden rule?

Eat things that expire faster than you.

Fresh food = longevity.

Processed food = your intestines waving a red flag.

And the best part?

Healthy old age is shockingly achievable. If you simply eat foods that your great-grandparents would recognize, you can become a cheerful old man (or woman) with absolutely no piles, no constipation, and no lifelong enemas scheduled every Monday.

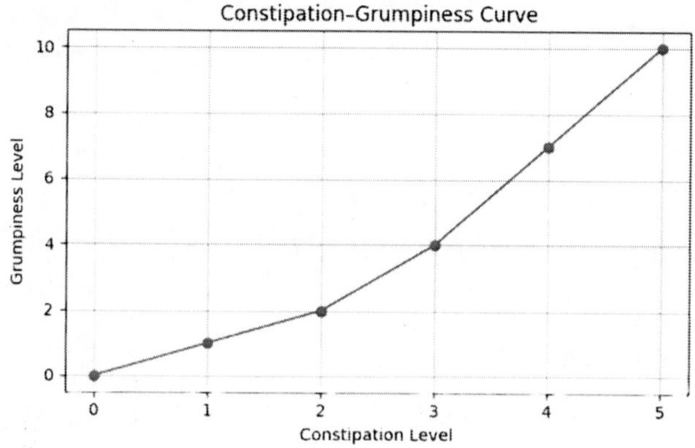

Most grumpy old people are not grumpy because they're old.

They're grumpy because nothing is moving inside them.

Their bowels are stuck.

Their moods are stuck.

Their entire personality is stuck.

Constipation is basically a hostage situation happening in the colon.

Half the key to mastering the art of dying lies in mastering the art of eating right.

Not spiritually, biologically.

Because what you eat for fifty years will silently decide how many pipes, tubes, wires, syringes, and medical contraptions will be attached to your body in the final chapter of your life.

If you ignore your diet now, modern medicine will happily insert technology into every available orifice later.

So eat well.

Eat smart.

Eat like someone who plans to age with dignity, not like someone auditioning to be a hospital mascot in retirement.

Your gut is your first brain.

Treat it like one.

Now back to just 'being.'

Just 'be'

You don't need to "build yourself."

You need to get out of your own damn way.

The more you try to become someone, the further you drift from the someone-less-ness that makes life sacred. Because when you stop trying to "be someone," you start being - *something.*

A presence.

A pulse.

A laugh in the void.

A witness to a moment that doesn't need a caption.

And isn't that enough?

Marcus Aurelius, the Roman Emperor who ruled half the world, once wrote to himself:

"You could leave life right now. Let that determine what you do, say, and think."

He didn't say this to depress himself.

He said it to wake up.

Because when you remember you're going to die, maybe not today, but definitely not today, the urge to perform for imaginary audiences suddenly feels exhausting.

Seneca, another delightful Stoic, called it what it is:

A waste of time trying to impress people who won't attend your funeral, and wouldn't recognise you in the casket even if they did.

To the Stoics, virtue was being aligned with one's own nature.

Not dressing it up. Not selling it.

Just... being.

"The Real" vs. "Trying to Be Real"

Trying to Be Real
Quick question: Should I wear the authentic linen or the raw hemp to my spiritual branding shoot?

The Real
You're naked under both, sweetheart.

Trying to Be Real

But people need to *feel* my truth, you know? Like, vibe with my journey. My wounds. My evolution.

The Real

Your "journey" is three playlists and a coffee addiction. Your wounds are mostly ego papercuts.

Trying to Be Real

Okay rude. I'm healing. I've done *the work*.

The Real

You've done the *presentation* of the work. You cried once during a podcast and called it a transformation.

Trying to Be Real

I just want to be my highest self.

The Real

There is no "high" self. You're not a ladder. You're who you are, and it's beautiful.

Trying to Be Real

But what if I don't become anyone?

The Real

Then maybe, finally, you'll become something

"You were born with nothing to prove, and yet you spend your life auditioning for ghosts. Die before the applause, and you might just hear silence applauding. Here, follow these 7 steps to be nothing:

How to Be Nothing in 7 Easy Steps

Finally, a step-by-step guide to complete spiritual irrelevance.

Step 1: Accept That You're Not Special

Repeat after me

"I am a limited edition snowflake made of the same atoms as dog hair and disappointment."

Now breathe. That's the universe exhaling your ego.

Step 2: Cancel Your Subscription to Meaning

Unsubscribe from the newsletter of significance.

Delete your inner life coach.

Block the algorithm that keeps asking you to find your purpose.

Spoiler: There isn't one. That's the gift.

Step 3: Fail Gracefully at Becoming Anyone

You tried.

You made a vision board.

You journaled with a fancy pen.

And yet, here you are, still undeniably you.

Perfect. Stay.

Step 4: Practice Radical Invisibility

Wear clothes that don't impress anyone.

Speak only when you mean it (you'll be quieter than a graveyard).

Watch how fast the world stops pretending to notice you.

Rejoice. You're free.

Step 5: Worship Dust

Find beauty in broken things.

Bow to trash bins.

Kiss the feet of the moment before the thought arrives.

Even God forgets to look holy on Fridays (Corporate Gods).

Step 6: Embrace the Glorious Uselessness of Being

Flowers don't justify their existence.

Rivers don't rush to career counselling.

Children don't cry because they haven't reached their "potential."

You, too, can be that stupidly sacred.

Step 7: Die Before You're Dead

Let the identity die.

Let the story collapse.

Let "you" become background noise.

Then notice

The breeze still moves,

The crow still shits on your car,

And the sun still rises,

Without anyone needing to become anything at all.

Congratulations!

You are now *Nothing*™.

Which is to say

Everything that never needed to be named

Once you taste that nothingness, you start to laugh, really laugh. Not the polite, social-media-approved laughter of "I'm fine," but the absurd kind that erupts when you realise there was no such thing as being someone, all along. The burden of being someone lifts, and what's left is just… being.

You no longer chase purpose; you play with it. You no longer seek validation; you watch it dissolve like sugar in tea. You start to see that the very meaning you were desperate to find was the very thing keeping you from living freely.

And that, my friend, is where the next revelation begins, not in discovering *more meaning,* but in finding joy in the lack of it.

Because when all illusions fade, when "you" finally take a back seat and life drives itself…

What remains is not despair.

It's laughter.

It's lightness.

It's **The Joy of Meaninglessness.**

Chapter - 4
Religion

Once upon a time, long before men in robes started building empires in the name of heaven. God was a whisper. A breeze through leaves. A sigh between stars. A silence so full it made the heart weep. But we were not content with whispers.

No.

We wanted certificates of divinity. Franchises of salvation. A trademark on the Infinite, with exclusive distribution rights to eternity, and, of course, a strict policy against outside snacks.

And so……. we created religion.

Not as a celebration, but as an enterprise. A bureaucratic pyramid scheme of holiness, complete with middlemen in robes and premium access to heaven. Millions followed, millions opposed, and somewhere in the corner, God wept. We never understood the simplest thing: God doesn't do group bookings. Divinity doesn't come in crowds; it gets drowned there. What thrives in masses isn't faith, it's theatre. A cheap production of pseudo-power, where the unemployed find purpose, the insecure find enemies, and everyone finds someone to blame.

Back home, the illusion collapses. Bills still need paying. Bellies still need feeding. The gods vanish until the next rally call, then the divine Wi-Fi reconnects. You march again, chest puffed, hashtag blessed, the fiercest soldier of your God…. And God, once a living presence, is now reduced to a product line. We replaced mystery with manuals, transcendence with merchandise, and called it devotion.

We burned forests to build temples. We took the cosmic joke of existence and turned it into a Sunday obligation with bad coffee and worse music. Where once God danced in rivers and laughed through children, He now sits like a bored bureaucrat in holy books, waiting to see who's wearing the right hat, eating the right food, and hating the right people.

God did not ruin life.

Religion did. When I was a child, my mother dragged me to one of those saints who had achieved the rare status of being both "renowned" and alive in central India. The ritual was simple: I was to touch his feet, as if my tiny palms could somehow vacuum up his accumulated holiness. I refused. I didn't know the man. Why should I caress his toes like a nervous devotee in a badly written mythological drama?

My mother, of course, was horrified. Her son had broken the sacred choreography of respect. She scolded me, as though I had just spat on the Vedas. But the saint surprised me. He didn't thunder with divine authority or strike me with a trident of enlightenment. Instead, he smiled. He called me closer, bent down, and whispered the only useful blessing I've ever received: *"Always question the things you do not understand."*

That was it. No mantras, no prophecies, no lifetime subscription to spiritual peace, just permission to question. And that single, ridiculous moment set the course of my life. I became a chronic sceptic, the kind of person who refuses to swallow scriptures whole, no matter how gold-leafed the cover. I don't care what gods allegedly said while floating on lotus petals; I prefer to check the footnotes, the fine print, and, if possible, the refund policy.

To this day, I only accept what convinces me after interrogation, preferably with a good lamp, a glass of water, and a cynical grin. If truth cannot withstand my questions, it deserves to collapse. If belief shivers when poked, it should. And maybe that was the real miracle of the saint: not that he gave me blessings, but that he handed me a weapon sharper than faith, doubt.

Religion, on the other hand, gives you the power to blindly renounce other religions and become a force so idiotic that you will wreak havoc on earth in its name. You will destroy everything that your sacred religion has said is not suited to your religions terms and conditions. You will also go blind and cast your vote to a party that promises to build concrete blocks that support your religious ideologies. You will stop caring about education, stop questioning human rights and stop engaging with people who do not support your ideology (blasphemous people). This is what religion has done. It has deepened the humanitarian divide. The world's happiest countries do not follow a particular religion. Instead, they are happy being "just humans" (Check out Finland).

The Sacred Is Not Serious

Here's the sick twist: Joy - spontaneous, purposeless, childlike joy- is now *suspicious.*

Laugh in a church, and you're disrespectful. Dance in a mosque and you're insane. Meditate without incense, and you're doing it wrong. The holy has become humourless. But real godliness, the kind that drips from moss, purrs in cats, and stares blankly at you from the eyes of a tired beggar, has no doctrine. It doesn't ask for rituals. It doesn't threaten you with afterlives. It doesn't care what you believe. It just *is.* And it's hilarious.

Because the idea that you must earn the right to live, to breathe, to feel joy, is the ultimate joke. You were *always* allowed to do that.

A Brief Summary of the Religious Experience (According to History)

Let's break down some of humanity's favourite salvation plans:

- **Christianity**

  Be born guilty for a sin you didn't commit, worship a tortured man nailed to wood, and hope a sky-father forgives you for masturbating.

- **Islam**

  Memorise a book you can't question, pray five times facing a cube, and if you die in the right war, you get women who never say no.

- **Hinduism**

  Thousands of gods, all of whom are angry, horny, or high. Die, be reborn, suffer again, unless you renounce pleasure, in which case… surprise! Enlightenment.

- **Buddhism**

  Life is suffering, desire is the cause, and nirvana is basically ghosting existence.

- **Judaism**

  A deeply philosophical people who argued with God until he left the group chat.

- **Modern Spirituality™**

  Crystals. Juice cleanses. Breathwork. Trust fund shamans who quote Rumi without ever feeling silence.

All these systems, in their sincere origins, were pointing at something real. But then came men. Men with pens, swords, microphones, and insecurities. They didn't want the truth. They wanted control. So God was domesticated. Divinity was weaponised. And joy became conditional. These Godmen taught us to fear them and be ready to be beheaded in the name of God. Be ready to offer wealth to God as and when He deems fit. Get a deal going with Him, 20% commission to God if He gets you the tender. Even more, sacrifice animals for His blessings and call it divine. Achieve such a level of divinity that you stop understanding the vastness of the universe, this existence, and start living in your own small world with your own God (who takes care of your business for a minor commission).

You think God is watching you? Judging you?

God isn't watching.

God *is* watching through your eyes.

Not as a judge, but as a guest.

Not as a punisher, but as a playmate.

The true God, if such a word still holds any weight, has no church, no scripture, no followers.

Only friends.

And most of them don't even know they're friends. They're too busy laughing at clouds, smelling the armpit of life, and being joyfully meaningless.

There was a time when humanity had a direct relationship with wonder.

We spoke to the stars without intermediaries. We bowed to trees without seeking permission.

We howled with wolves and wept with rivers. But then came the middlemen. Men who claimed they had God's WhatsApp number. Men who wore funny hats, recited memorised threats, and demanded that you stop thinking and start donating. These were not sages. They were spiritual landlords charging rent on land they never owned. And like good little seekers, we handed over the deed to our lives. We obeyed. We sacrificed. We gave them power they didn't earn and reverence they didn't deserve.

Let's be brutally honest

Many of the world's most beloved religious leaders wouldn't pass a basic ethics test.

Forget enlightenment, some can't even spell it.

They sit on thrones of gold, preaching poverty. They sell heaven in exchange for obedience.

They promise salvation while harbouring scandal.

And the irony?

Their followers defend them *even harder* when the mask slips.

Because nothing is more terrifying to the devout than realising the "holy man" is just a lonely man with a God complex and a tax-free income.

We've turned charisma into credibility, costumes into credentials, and rituals into rackets.

Modern Humanity: A Cautionary Tale in Three Acts

Act I: Born free, curious, wild.

Act II: Taught shame, guilt, obedience.

Told to fear our own joy.

Told that pleasure was suspicious, laughter was vulgar, and dancing was demonic.

Act III: Grows up. Goes to therapy.

Starts to *unlearn* religion and accidentally rediscovers God hiding in an avocado.

Meanwhile, Nature Weeps (But Also Laughs)

The trees look at us and sigh,

"Really? You made paper to write commandments that said we were less important than a bearded man in the sky?"

The rivers ask,

"Why do you pollute us and then sprinkle us on babies in the name of purification?"

The animals, oh, the animals.

They've been watching for centuries,

Wondering how the apex predator with nuclear weapons is scared of premarital sex.

The animals eat, sleep, mate, and die, without moral footnotes, without hashtags, without therapy sessions to forgive their parents.

They don't fear judgment, because they never outsourced their instincts to ideology.

And perhaps that's what makes them free. They live without the constant need to "become" something. They just are.

While we, the great *Homo sapiens,* bury our simplicity under ambition, guilt, and God. The animals must look at us and whisper,

"Poor things… they evolved too far and forgot how to live."

Because somewhere along the evolutionary highway, we took a wrong turn, straight into organised confusion. We invented middlemen between ourselves and the divine, priests with microphones louder than God's silence, translators who charge a fee to interpret eternity. We stopped thinking and started outsourcing our souls to anyone wearing saffron, white, green, or a fake smile.

Illiteracy didn't just rob us of reading; it robbed us of reasoning. And now, even the literate have joined the ranks of the unthinking, scrolling instead of studying, preaching instead of understanding. Common sense has become so uncommon that it should be declared an endangered species.

And this, right here, is where the comedy turns into tragedy. Because the less we think, the more we believe. The fewer questions we ask, the holier the answers sound.

***

Faith without Thought: The Glorious March of the Uneducated Devotee

Education is dangerous.

It encourages questions.

And nothing threatens blind faith more than a question asked sincerely.

Which is why, for centuries, religious establishments made a sport of burning books, silencing thinkers, and calling curiosity a sin. Because once you teach a child to read, they might just stumble upon the fact that the earth doesn't need saving, we do.

They might ask

- Why does God need a spokesperson who can't spell?
- Why is the afterlife more important than actual life?
- And why do these holy men seem to enjoy controlling women's bodies more than their own urges?

Of course, that would be a problem.

Because religion thrives best in ignorance, not the innocent kind, but the cultivated, stubborn kind.

The kind that clutches scriptures with bloodied hands and shouts "truth" over the cries of the dying.

History isn't shy.

It's just unread by the faithful.

In the name of peace, we've waged unholy wars.

In the name of love, we've burned children alive.

In the name of God, we've erased civilisations and still dared to sing hymns afterwards.

- **Crusades:** A centuries-long exercise in divine genocide.
- **Inquisitions:** Torture chambers with Bible verses etched into the walls.

- **Jihads:** Explosions wrapped in scriptures and shame.
- Holy lynchings, witch burnings, temple riots, all done by men too proud to read a science book but well-versed in celestial punishment.

There is no corner of the earth untouched by blood spilt for belief.

And the greatest irony?

The men who kill for God often don't know the first thing about life. They speak of heaven with the precision of a travel agent, but have never watched a sunset without turning it into scripture. They worship death as a ticket to salvation, yet have never truly lived enough to appreciate a breath. They kill in the name of peace, rage in the name of love, and condemn others in the name of their so - called "true God." These men talk about divinity, but their eyes never soften at a child's laughter. They preach compassion but cannot feed a hungry dog. God, poor God, has become their hostage, a convenient mascot for every fear they refuse to face. He's been dragged into parliaments, wars, WhatsApp groups, and dinner arguments, forced to pick sides in conflicts He never started. The Almighty, once infinite, is now reduced to a logo - printed, copyrighted, and weaponised.

If there is suffering in heaven, it must be His, watching His name inked on bombs and banknotes alike, wondering how His creation learned to pray louder than it learned to live. And just when He thinks the noise might settle, humanity finds a new way to disappoint Him by dragging half the species into guilt for existing.

Because when men couldn't understand God, they decided to control women instead. It was simpler. You can't silence the divine, but you can silence the one who gives birth to life.

Women: The First Casualties of Male Spiritual Insecurity

Ah, women, the original sin, according to some.

Temptresses, witches, womb-bearers, liabilities.

In the hands of ignorant men drunk on God and testosterone, women were turned into breeding machines, property, and moral scapegoats.

The logic went something like this

1. A woman spoke her mind → she's dangerous.
2. A woman enjoyed sex → she's evil.
3. A woman didn't obey → she's possessed.
4. A woman led → she's a blasphemer in heels.

For centuries, women have been

- Locked up for being curious.
- Burned for being beautiful.
- Silenced for being wise.
- Blamed for being human.

And all the while, the men, these self-proclaimed "spiritual leaders"

Could barely read, couldn't control their desires, and thought enlightenment was something you inherited by sitting on the right cushion.

They built entire systems of worship where women could serve, but never speak.

Where they could cover their faces, but not uncover the truth.

Where their worth began at virginity and ended at obedience.

Where devotion was measured not by love, but by silence.

For centuries, the divine feminine was edited out of the narrative, replaced by rules, rituals, and the fragile egos of men who mistook control for holiness. They feared women because women didn't need temples to feel God; they could bleed, give birth, and still nurture life, miracles men could only preach about. And so, patriarchy had to dress itself in bullshit and call it spirituality.

But suppression has evolved, like everything else.

We've upgraded from stone altars to digital platforms. The same old ignorance now wears modern robes, polyester instead of cotton, Wi-Fi instead of incense. It no longer hides behind temples; it goes live on YouTube.

Modern Day Idiocy: Now with Wi-Fi and Holy Apps

Today, the weapons have changed, but the war remains.

Ignorance still wears a robe. It now livestreams sermons.

It spreads hatred through hashtags and monetizes outrage by the minute.

What used to be shouted from pulpits is now whispered through algorithms, faster, louder, and more profitable

Issues fatwas with a ring light and a Patreon.

The educated are suspicious. The reflective are mocked. The spiritual-but-not-stupid are still fringe.

And the women?

Still told how to dress, how to pray, how to shrink.

By men whose only spiritual achievement is memorising what another uneducated man once said - loudly.

A Dialogue Between "The Blind Believer" and "The Girl He Burned at the Stake"

*[**Setting:** A shadowy realm where time has no meaning. The charred scent of memory hangs in the air. A man in tattered robes clutches a holy book with trembling hands. A girl, radiant in the quiet glow of what should have been, steps forward, barefoot, whole, and very much alive.]*

Blind Believer

You...

You can't be here.

You're supposed to be gone. Cleansed. Purged in holy fire.

Girl

And yet, here I am.

Unburned.

Unlike your brain, which seems thoroughly well-done.

Blind Believer

I did what I was told.

You spoke to birds. You danced under the moon.

You... you didn't bow.

Girl

I know.

Terrifying, isn't it? A woman existing without permission.

Blind Believer

You were dangerous! The clergy agreed.

They said you were possessed.

Girl

I was.

With wonder.

With laughter.

With the unbearable lightness of not giving a damn about your angry little gods.

Blind Believer

We had rules. Sacred laws. You broke them.

Girl

And you broke me.

To pieces.

To ash.

Then swept me under the altar like spilled wine.

Blind Believer

But… I believed. I followed the righteous path!

Girl

You followed a man who hadn't bathed in a decade and thought menstrual blood was Satan's ink.

Let's not pretend it was righteousness.

Blind Believer

I feared God!

Girl

Exactly.

And so you feared joy, freedom, music, curiosity, women, dancing, mirrors, and your own shadow.

You weren't devout.

You were *terrified.*

Blind Believer

But the scripture!

Girl

Was written by men who couldn't explain lightning,

But felt confident deciding the fate of my soul.

Blind Believer

I thought I was saving you.

Girl

You were saving yourself.

From the terrifying idea that maybe…

You were wrong.

That maybe God doesn't care how I braid my hair

Or which direction you face when you kneel.

That maybe, just maybe,

The divine doesn't wear robes or speak in threats.

That maybe God was in the laugh you silenced,

In the questions you feared,

And yes, even in my dance under the moon.

Blind Believer

So what now? Am I damned?

Girl

Oh sweetheart.

There is no hell but the one you built in your own mind and dragged the rest of us into.

Blind Believer

And you? Are you free?

Girl

I was always free.

You just mistook it for rebellion.

Because to a man in chains, freedom always looks dangerous

EULOGY FOR RELIGION

(As delivered by a sceptical child and an over qualified tree.)

Child (age 7, unbaptized and suspicious):

We are gathered here today to say goodbye to religion, that great and terrible babysitter of the human soul.

Born in fear, raised in guilt, and survived mostly through threats,

Religion lived a long, manipulative life.

It promised salvation but delivered segregation.

It claimed love, but only if you read the fine print.

And it built empires, on bones, blood, and bad translations.

Tree (6,000 years old, speaks in rustling):

I watched it all.

From crucifixions to holy wars,

From temples turned banks to popes turned influencers.

Religion climbed the highest mountains

Not to find God,

But to claim a better reception for its doctrine.

Child

It convinced billions that God was male,

Those women were sinning with legs,

And that heaven was gated, guarded, and available

Only to those who subscribed to the correct invisible friend.

Tree

It made people kneel when they should have danced.

It made them confess what they didn't need forgiveness for

And carry guilt like sacred luggage.

Child

But now...

Religion has passed.

Choked on its own dogma,

Strangled by the irony of claiming absolute truth in a universe made entirely of change.

Let us not weep.

Let us remember Religion for what it *tried* to be,

A bridge to the infinite

That somehow became a toll booth run by small, angry men.

Tree

Let us bury it deep.

In compost.

So perhaps something honest might grow from it at last.

Obituary

Religion, aged several millennia, passed away peacefully in the minds of the thoughtful.

It is survived by spiritual curiosity, wonder, and the overwhelming mystery of existence.

In place of flowers, please plant questions in your mind and water them with doubt.

A wake will be held in silence, under the stars, where no sermon will be given, and no guilt will be served.

***

Final Words at the Graveside

And as the casket is lowered

May we throw in the fear,

The shame,

The unearned authority,

And all the small-minded certainties that kept humans from seeing godliness in themselves.

Let the tombstone read

"Here lies Religion - it died as it lived: loudly, hypocritically, and utterly confused."

Chapter - 5

The Myth of Purpose - Memento Mori, Memento Vivere

" The two most important days in your life are the day you are born and the day you find out it didn't matter."

Mark Twain, probably while chain-smoking and watching the Mississippi dry up

Enter the Grand Stage of Cosmic Comedy

In a universe so vast that your entire life fits into the sneeze of a dying star, we humans have developed a wonderful coping mechanism: Purpose. The great sugar-coated illusion. The scented candle of existential dread. The emotional support animal of the terrified ego.

Mark Twain chuckled at mankind's obsession with finding meaning. Aristotle philosophized about virtue and reason while also owning slaves. Machiavelli told us the end justifies the means, right before being politically exiled. And Alexander the Great? He wept because there were no more lands to conquer, though rumour has it, he hadn't even conquered himself.

Let us now bow to the great human tradition of wanting things to matter.

But first: Memento Mori - remember that you will die. A beautiful Latin phrase often engraved on tombstones, motivational Instagram posts, and the forearms of men who drink espresso with rum.

But today, dear reader, I invite you to upgrade.

You see - if you're going to die anyway, why not dance badly in the meantime? Why not create a world around you where nobody judges anybody, where happiness isn't a performance but a state of being? Why not surround yourself with people who are innately alive, not endlessly rehearsing for some cosmic audition?

Here's a radical idea: reverse-engineer your death. Imagine the moment you're about to leave this world. Where are you? What are you doing? Who's around you, if anyone at all? My answer is "I want to die teaching," then I would want to live in a way that my final breath could actually find me in a classroom, mid-sentence, sharing something that matters. If you want to die painting, start painting now. If you want to die at peace, stop waging wars, internal or external, today.

Most people die without ever deciding how they want to die. They're so busy "building a future" they forget to build a present worth dying in. So live backwards. Start at the end. Work your life like a blueprint of your deathbed, not your bank account. Stop hoarding legacies for people who won't remember you beyond three generations. Start collecting moments you'd want to carry into oblivion. That is the quiet, radical rebellion: to live in such a way that death finds you exactly where you wanted to be, doing exactly what you wanted to do; no applause, no audience, just you, fulfilled.

Alexander the Great's Final Inventory Report

Location: Babylon, 323 BCE

Status: Conquered the known world

Mood: Surprisingly empty

Final Possessions

- A sword
- A lot of sand
- Regret
- Dysentery

Legend says Alexander requested to be buried with his hands dangling outside his coffin, to show the world he was leaving with nothing. Beautiful, poetic, and also extremely impractical for coffin logistics.

But oh, how that image lingers: the world's greatest conqueror... with empty palms. Like a man who spent his whole life building the ultimate LEGO set only to be told he can't take it home.

We've been sold the idea that life must have a singular, glowing "purpose," as though we're born with a mission statement etched somewhere in our DNA. We chase it like a coupon for eternity, believing that if we just "find our calling," everything else will fall into place. But the joke's on us: purpose has become the last refuge of the ego.

Purpose is static. It's a banner you wave. A PowerPoint you show investors. A mantra you repeat to yourself so you feel significant. Consciousness, on the other hand, is fluid. It evolves. It doesn't ask you to declare who you are; it quietly changes who you are.

Look at the so-called greats. Gandhi didn't come out of the womb with a salt march in his hands. Buddha didn't start by renouncing kingdoms; he started by living in one. Oppenheimer didn't build an atomic bomb because it was his "purpose," he built it because he read and understood theoretical physics, then spent the rest of his life questioning what he'd done. Even the Wright Brothers weren't born to "redefine mobility." They just kept tinkering with bicycles until their curiosity took flight.

None of these people "found" a purpose. They lived, stumbled, learned, evolved, and their rising consciousness shaped what they eventually did. Their actions were an *outcome* of their awareness, not a pre-written script. They didn't start with grand visions. They started with questions, with confusion, with curiosity.

And that's the thing: living with higher consciousness isn't about meditating on a mountain or chanting Sanskrit verses until your ego dies. It's about noticing, really noticing, how you think, how you act, how you affect others. It's about letting your life transform you rather than trying to bend life to fit your self-imposed purpose.

Purpose is a destination; consciousness is a journey. Purpose ends with a trophy, a book, a statue, or a hashtag. Consciousness never ends; it keeps expanding until the idea of a "trophy" seems comical.

So forget trying to stamp your name on the universe. Forget carving your "legacy" into the cosmic guestbook. The universe doesn't do monuments; it does motion. The real work isn't to "find your purpose." The real work is to live in a state of ever-rising awareness, so whatever you do, teach, build, march, invent, or just sit still, is a natural outpouring of who you've become, not a performance for history.

Because, in the end, purpose will die with you. Consciousness, though, even if only for a moment, makes you truly alive.

So What Now?

The stars don't know your name.

The oceans do not care for your productivity hacks.

And Death, our sarcastic, patient friend, sits sipping wine, waiting for your next great life plan to collapse in a heap of hilarious disappointment.

So what should you do?

Laugh.

Live.

Make a joke in poor taste.

Love someone who isn't useful to your career.

Because when the myth of purpose dies, play begins.

Final Aphorisms from the Tombstone Carver

- "He tried to leave a legacy. Mostly left laundry."
- "She followed her passion. It filed a restraining order."
- "They died with purpose. Death didn't care."
- "I lived once. It was overrated. But at least I danced."

What is the purpose of a rose blooming?

None. It just does. Unapologetically. Senselessly. Beautifully. It doesn't write a blog about "10 Tips to Bloom Authentically." It simply exists. Then it wilts. And nobody holds a funeral.

What is the purpose of a fish swimming peacefully?

None. It doesn't go to a seminar. It doesn't feel ashamed for not being a shark. It doesn't compare gills on LinkedIn. It just *is*.

You, however, have been convinced that you must *become* something.

A CEO. A monk. A TED speaker. A "fulfilled soul."

The irony? In all your striving to become someone, you slowly stop being.

Museum of Dead Purposes

Now, let me take you on a brief tour.

To your left, the Exhibit of Abandoned Callings, here lies the skeleton of a man who tried to change the world through spreadsheets.

On your right, the Gallery of Burnt-Out Yogis, each gave up wine, sex, and sugar... only to die constipated and bitter.

And in the centre, behold the Shrine of Unread Journals, filled with desperate affirmations like

- "I am enough."
- "I will manifest abundance."
- "I forgive Steve for not texting back."

They all died eventually. Some are still manifesting. None particularly abundant.

The tragedy of purpose is that it gives your life no meaning at all. If you achieve it, you're done, the curtain falls, applause fades, and you're left awkwardly standing on stage, unsure what to do with your hands. If you fail, you're shattered, convinced you've wasted your existence. Either way, you're trapped in a loop of self-importance. Purpose is the carrot life dangles in front of the ego to keep it running on the treadmill of "becoming."

Nobody tells you that the carrot was plastic.

What if the goal isn't to *become* anything at all, but to simply *be*; alert, alive, unfiltered? Living, not as a career choice, but as an art form. You don't paint to finish the canvas; you paint because the brush feels right in your hand. You don't dance to arrive somewhere; you dance because stillness becomes unbearable. That's life, movement without motive.

Humans, however, can't stop writing resumes for existence. We turn life into an internship under Death's supervision. We make five-year plans for something that has no guarantee of five minutes.

The Pointless Beauty of Living

Living, in its purest form, has no agenda. You breathe not to achieve respiration goals, but because the alternative is inconvenient. You smile not because you planned to, but because something in the absurd chaos made sense for half a second.

Life only becomes meaningful when you stop trying to make it meaningful. When you stop decorating it with slogans and start laughing at the circus of it all. When you stop asking *"What am I supposed to do?"* and start asking *"How can I simply be?"*

Because when living itself becomes the purpose, everything you do, from sipping chai to screwing up gloriously, becomes sacred. You're no longer in a race; you're in rhythm. The meaning of life is not a destination. It's the music you create without knowing the notes.

How to Live (A Briefly Unauthorised Guide)

Osho once said, "Don't seek meaning, dance. Don't seek God, laugh." Which, of course, instantly got turned into a printed poster and sold at gift shops by people who did neither.

Living is not a discipline; it's a rebellion. You don't live correctly. You live completely. Krishnamurti said, "It is no measure of health to be well-adjusted to a profoundly sick society." Yet here we are, scheduling mindfulness between sales calls.

How to live? Start by disappointing expectations, especially your own. Refuse to optimise your soul. Don't let your morning routine become your religion. Skip the gratitude journal once in a while and binge-watch a serial killer series, or MasterChef, whatever. Nobody will judge you, except you. If you must have a purpose, let it be to live with awareness, not the filtered, social-media awareness of "living my best life," but the raw, unedited kind that occasionally smells like panic and tea.

To live well is not to be perpetually happy. It's to be perpetually *awake*. To laugh at your illusions, to cry without reason, to forget your image long enough to feel something real.

Joy as Rebellion

Joy is not entertainment. It's defiance. It's what remains when the world fails to make you bitter. Most people think joy is the reward of meaning. It's the other way around; joy gives life meaning.

A truly joyful person is society's worst nightmare. You can't manipulate them with fear or reward. They don't vote for messiahs. They don't join causes just to post about them. They laugh in temples, forgive without ceremony, and find beauty in Pineapple toppings on a pizza.

When you live joyfully, you become untouchable, not because you've conquered suffering, but because you've stopped taking it personally. Joy doesn't mean the absence of sorrow; it means you stopped renting it a room.

Krishnamurti would say that joy is the fragrance of understanding. Osho would add that it's the laughter of awareness. Both were right. Joy is not an emotion; it's an intelligence, the wisdom to see that everything, even tragedy, has its comic timing.

Imagine a world where people didn't chase meaning, but created moments. Where instead of collecting possessions, they collected laughter. Where sharing joy was the only social currency that mattered.

You wouldn't need religion, because compassion would be instinctive. You wouldn't need therapy, because you'd have community. You wouldn't need legacy, because every moment would feel eternal.

Yes, it sounds utopian. It also sounds ridiculous. But so does everything worth doing.

The great cosmic joke is that happiness doesn't come from purpose, achievement, or enlightenment. It comes from the simplest rebellion of all, being fully, foolishly, consciously alive.

The Cult of Productivity

(Where busy people go to die slowly)

If there is one religion modern humans truly follow, it is Productivity. Not Hinduism, not Islam, not Christianity, not Buddhism.

The real god is Efficiency, the real prayer is "I'm so busy." And the real temple is a Google Calendar that looks like a toddler scribbled on it with crayons.

People treat being busy as a personality trait.

Not busy *doing what*, mind you.

Just busy, existentially, spiritually, chronically.

It's the only socially accepted form of suffering you're allowed to brag about.

Ask someone, "How are you?" They'll sigh dramatically and announce,

"I'm *so* busy."

This translates to

"I need you to know I'm important, even though I'm dead inside."

The Cult of Productivity wants you to believe that if you aren't constantly grinding, hustling, optimising your routine, and waking up at 4:00 AM like a deranged rooster, you are wasting your life.

Sleep is weakness.

Rest is laziness.

Joy is unproductive.

Even burnout has become a badge of honour.

People proudly say things like

"I haven't slept properly in three years,"

As if they're describing a noble pilgrimage rather than slowly committing emotional suicide.

Your worth has been reduced to how well you perform like a machine.

The irony?

Machines take breaks.

Humans don't.

They "push through."

They "give 200%."

They "crush goals."

They "optimise workflows."

And then they crash into a therapist's couch, weeping into recycled tissue paper.

Productivity has the same old claim: "You have the same 24 hours as Beyoncé."

No, you don't.

She has a staff of 120.

You have acid reflux and two pending electricity bills.

The high priests of productivity wear fitness trackers, drink mushroom-infused coffee, and confuse being awake with being alive.

They track every step, heartbeat, bowel movement, minute of REM sleep, not because they want to live well, but because they are terrified of being less important.

They want to upgrade themselves into some premium version of humanity:

Human 2.0, Now With Less Emotion and More Output™

Somewhere along the way, "being" stopped mattering and "doing" became the only acceptable form of existence.

You don't walk anymore; you track steps.

You don't relax anymore; you optimise recovery.

You don't sit in silence anymore; you meditate to increase productivity.

Even leisure has become scheduled:

"Monday 8:00–8:30 PM: Enjoy life."

A calendar invitation goes out.

Five people decline.

One accepts but joins late due to network issues.

Krishnamurti must be laughing silently in his grave.

The man who tried to teach the world freedom from conditioning would be horrified to see humans willingly enrolling in Self-Improvement Slavery™.

Workplaces: The Modern Gulags of the Soul

Ah, the workplace, the sanitised, air-conditioned concentration camp for creativity.

Managers keep you "aligned" like a chiropractor for the spirit.

Your KPI becomes the measure of your existence, your appraisal the judgment day of your soul.

Workplaces say things like

"We are a family."

Translation

"You can't leave without guilt."

They pretend to care about mental health by organizing mandatory "Well-being Workshops" on Saturdays at 9 AM.

Someone talks about "striking a balance," while HR silently updates your attendance record.

People spend their entire lives chasing promotions that only promote their suffering.

They retire with a watch, a cake, and decades of unexpressed emotion — then die of loneliness while their company replaces them within six business hours.

This is the Cult of Productivity.

A global hallucination convincing you that your value is equal to your output.

That rest is a sin.

That your life is a project plan.

That your heart is a furnace meant to burn endlessly without maintenance.

The Alternative: Being Useless (Beautifully)

Here's the forbidden truth:

Life does not give a single damn about your productivity.

The universe is expanding at 70 kilometres per second per megaparsec.

Stars are collapsing.

Galaxies are being born.

Nebulas are exploding.

Meanwhile, you're worried about clearing 12 emails before lunch.

Do you see the comedy?

The cosmic absurdity?

To live well, you must be brave enough to be useless sometimes.

Useless to capitalism.

Useless to your job title.

Useless to people who expect you to perform like a circus animal.

Sit.

Breathe.

Stare at a plant.

Watch a pigeon do nothing for 45 minutes.

Let your neurosis scream.

Look at your office problem again.

No solution??

Then ignore it.

The point is not to be lazy about it.

The point is to give it time. And to you, too. Chances are, it will sort itself out. If not, sit again with the problem. Repeat. But no need to lose sleep over it.

Osho said, "A flower does not bloom to serve."

And you, my friend, are not an industry.

You are an organism.

A messy, unpredictable, gloriously inefficient organism.

Stop worshipping productivity.

Start worshipping awareness.

Start worshipping joy.

Start worshipping the freedom to exist without justification.

Because the day you die:

(And trust me, HR cannot stop that meeting)

Your to-do list will still have items pending.

Your inbox will still have unread emails.

Your team will still schedule a follow-up.

But you?

You will finally be free of the greatest scam humanity ever invented,

That you must *earn* your right to exist

So laugh. Dance. Cry. Trip over your own philosophies. Love badly. Forgive accidentally.

And when you die, die mid-laughter, preferably at the absurdity of ever taking yourself so seriously.

Chapter - 6

Why Dying Young is not the Problem, Living Half-Dead is

Modern humans are obsessed with not dying.

They count steps. Track sleep. Monitor heart rates, gut bacteria, glucose spikes, emotional well-being. They drink green liquids that taste like regret and speak reverently about longevity as if death might reconsider if the correct supplements are taken at the correct time of day.

And yet, despite all this effort, most people look exhausted.

We are living longer, yes, but not necessarily living. We have perfected the science of keeping bodies alive while quietly anaesthetizing the spirit. Lifespan has increased. Vitality has not. A remarkable achievement, medically speaking. A tragic one, existentially.

The problem is not dying young.

The problem is spending decades alive while feeling vaguely sedated.

Somewhere along the way, longevity became the goal. Not aliveness. Not curiosity. Not intensity. Just duration. As if staying on the planet longer, regardless of how, were inherently virtuous.

Nobody asks the obvious question: Alive how?

Because that question is inconvenient. It demands honesty instead of discipline. Presence instead of planning.

A man who dies at forty after living fiercely, laughing deeply, choosing courage over comfort is considered tragic. A man who lives to ninety while hating his mornings, fearing his evenings, suppressing his desires, and waiting patiently for weekends that never deliver is considered successful.

This tells you everything you need to know about modern values.

We have confused survival with living.

And yet, history has an inconvenient habit of refusing to cooperate with this obsession.

Some people died young, and somehow refuse to die.

Swami Vivekananda lived only thirty-nine years. Long enough to wake a sleeping civilisation, short enough to avoid becoming its mascot. He burned intensely and left before his fire could be diluted into slogans.

Bhagat Singh did not reach thirty. He had no interest in longevity, no patience for safety, no fascination with legacy. He lived awake in a time that punished wakefulness.

Alexander conquered the known world before most people today finish figuring out their five-year plans. He died at thirty-two, unfinished, exhausted, already mythic, not because he lived long, but because he lived fully implicated in his ambition.

Kurt Cobain left before rebellion could become nostalgia. He felt too much in a world that rewards numbness. Decades later, his voice still sounds more alive than most people comfortably surviving into middle age.

Ayrton Senna raced as if death were already in the passenger seat, not recklessly, but honestly. Presence at full speed. No postponement.

Heath Ledger disappeared before the industry could explain him away. He left a disturbance, not a résumé.

What unites these lives is not early death.

It is the absence of dilution.

They did not live long enough to become cautious. They did not trade intensity for safety. They did not postpone vitality in exchange for time. They died young, but not half-dead.

And yet, and honesty demands this, dying young is not a prerequisite for living fully.

Some people lived long and still refused to go numb.

Leonardo da Vinci lived into old age and died unfinished, still curious, still sketching, still asking questions. Time did not tame him.

Michelangelo lived nearly ninety years, arguing with popes, climbing scaffolds, carving marble with undiminished fury. Longevity did not soften him. It sharpened him.

Picasso lived past ninety and never stopped reinventing himself, artistically, emotionally, chaotically. Whatever his flaws, half-dead was not one of them.

Nelson Mandela survived decades of confinement without letting bitterness become his identity. He did not merely endure life; he re-entered it.

What separates these lives from the quietly numbed majority is not genetics, discipline, or supplements.

It is engagement.

They did not live long, instead of being alive.

They lived long while being alive.

They did not postpone curiosity.

They did not dilute passion for safety.

They did not confuse aging with surrender.

So this is not an argument against longevity.

It is an argument against postponement.

Against the belief that you will live later, once things settle, once security arrives, once conditions improve. That "later" is the most efficient way to die slowly.

Longevity without vitality is not wisdom.

It is endurance.

Vitality with longevity is rare, but when it happens, it exposes the lie completely.

Life does not reward time served.

It responds to presence.

The tragedy is not dying young.

The tragedy is mistaking survival for participation, and congratulating ourselves for it.

Chapter - 7
Why Am I?

(The Most Important Question You Will Ever Be Terrified to Ask)

The Forbidden Question

Every meaningful revolution in human consciousness begins with a question.

Not a great war.

Not a religious awakening.

Not a TED Talk delivered by a man in a black turtleneck who says "synergy" too often.

No, but a question.

But not all questions were born equal.

Some questions are harmless, like

- "Where are my keys?"
- "Did I lock the door?"
- "What happens if I microwave foil?"

These questions may destroy your house, but never your worldview.

Then there is the most domesticated, overused spiritual question of all time, the one that has been neutered by centuries of misuse:

"Who am I?"

This question is the emotional equivalent of a stress ball.

Squeeze it, poke it, meditate on it, attend 14 retreats about it, and you still return to work on Monday morning only slightly more confused.

"Who am I?" is socially acceptable existentialism.

It is philosophy in a seatbelt.

It is the spiritual question religions *want* you to ask because it keeps you busy but obedient.

But then… There is the forbidden question.

The nuclear question.

The question with the philosophical blast radius of an exploding sun:

"Why am I?"

The moment this question enters your nervous system, your old worldview begins to glitch like a Windows 98 computer.

It destabilises religion.

It threatens governments.

It neutralises motivational speakers.

It confuses therapists.

It terrifies your boss.

It disables the economy for at least three days.

If too many people started asking "Why am I?" sincerely, the global GDP would drop by 76% before lunch.

Society depends on you *not* asking this question.

Your survival in the system requires you to remain existentially sedated.

That's why "Who am I?" is encouraged.

And "Why am I?" is avoided like a contagious philosophical disease.

The Birthplace of Why - Childhood, Conditioning, and the Accident of Consciousness

Children do not ask, "Why am I?"

They ask questions that actually matter:

Why is the sky blue?

Why can't I eat cake for breakfast?

Why does Dad look sad after checking his email?

Why does Mom whisper-cry in the bathroom?

Children ask questions that reveal truths adults have learned to hide.

But as you grow, society replaces inquiry with conditioning

- Sit straight.
- Study this.
- Become that.
- Don't ask why.
- Follow instructions.
- Don't embarrass the family.
- Don't dream too much.
- Don't question the teacher.

By adolescence, you have forgotten the most important question entirely.

You replace it with:

"Will they like me?"

"Am I attractive?"

"What career should I choose?"

"How much do engineers earn?"

"How do I become successful?"

These questions feed the system.

But "Why am I?"

Ah, that question would lead you out of the system.

And so society kills it early.

Education doesn't answer it.

Religion oversimplifies it.

Parents avoid it.

Capitalism monetises it.

Therapy postpones it.

Philosophy complicates it.

And then suddenly, one night at 2:17 AM, after too many heartbreaks and a suspicious transaction alert from your bank, the question returns like an uninvited guest:

"Why am I?"

And it hits you with a force no childhood conditioning can suppress.

At this point, Camus would say you have finally become conscious. Not awakened. Not enlightened. Just painfully aware. Aware that the universe is not whispering instructions. Aware that existence, despite centuries of prayer, philosophy, and desperate journaling, refuses to explain itself.

The silence is not poetic.

It is indifferent.

Almost rude.

Humans do not tolerate silence well. We crave reasons the way addicts crave fixes. We smash our heads against the cosmic wall, demanding meaning from something that never promised to provide it. The wall, as expected, does not respond.

This collision- between your hunger for meaning and the universe's refusal to cooperate- is what Camus called the absurd. A creature desperate for explanation living inside a reality that does not care enough to explain itself. Most people hear this and collapse into despair. Others panic and sprint back to borrowed narratives, religion, success, productivity, anything that offers the illusion of coherence.

Camus did something more offensive.

He shrugged.

If life comes without inherent meaning, then it also comes without cosmic obligation. You are not failing an assignment. You are not late. You are not disappointing the universe. The universe is not watching. And that realisation, unsettling as it is, carries an unexpected gift.

Freedom.

But freedom, it turns out, is not comforting.

Freedom is heavy. Freedom cages you into believing you are above everyone else. It gives you a certain confidence that may feel liberating at the start, but slowly starts taking the shape of a burden. It creates an illusion of being powerful. What freedom is a careful realisation of the fact that there is nothing to be taken for granted, nothing to be expected from anyone and most definitely nothing to be afraid of. We mistake freedom with financial independence, or not being answerable to anyone (yes, but you are answerable to yourself). You need to ask yourself: Am I free, or am I pretending to be free?

Kafka would have understood this immediately. He would not have waited for freedom to arrive; he would have recognised it as an endless corridor of doors, each promising clarity, each opening into yet another waiting room. You move through education, careers, relationships, and spiritual systems with quiet optimism, convinced that the next door will finally explain your presence.

It never does.

And slowly, uncomfortably, the realisation settles in: perhaps there was never meant to be an explanation. Your freedom was already approved by existence itself. The waiting rooms were your own construction, carefully built to delay the moment you stop asking for permission.

This is unbearable at first. Humans are not built for ambiguity. We want a function, a role, a designation. Something neat. Something defensible. Something we can point to when the question gets aggressive. Like when a man is not earning, he is not good enough. When a woman is not cooking, she is not good enough. If you are single at 40, you have not played by the rules set out by society. If you are divorced at 40 and living happily, you must be having illicit affairs. Otherwise, how can you be happy without a family? We have so much societal baggage that it is nearly impossible to be accepted the way we want to exist. So we camouflage ourselves into men and women of high order (as society would see it). We start wearing branded outfits (no harm in that, but for societal acceptance? Nahh), we start posting our happiness on Instagram (as if anybody cares), we start quoting big philosophers for acceptance amongst intellectuals (like I am doing). All this is a façade. An acceptance of our scared little minds that keeps questioning us: "What if society does not accept me?" That is when we start looking for purpose. We seek purpose to fit in. To be accepted. To be of some value to society. Not for its value, but to be praised by society.

This is where the ancient comfort sneaks in, the idea that everything must have a purpose because it feels safer that way. That knives cut, seeds grow, and humans, by virtue of thinking, must be meant for something exceptional.

Aristotle once believed this with admirable confidence.

But Aristotle never met a modern human.

If Aristotle were alive today, watching people attend "purpose workshops" while avoiding their own lives, he might quietly revise his theory and admit: humans are the only species intelligent enough to sabotage being alive.

The purpose of a tree is not to give oxygen. It simply exists. And in the quiet, uncelebrated act of existing, it keeps humans alive. We repay this generosity by cutting it down to wipe our shitty asses. A touching exchange. A masterclass in gratitude. We turned our life-giver into a toilet flush.

And yet, the tree keeps giving.

Not because it understands morality. Not because it is enlightened. But because it does not know it is being useful. It does not know it is saving lives. It is free from the burden of purpose.

There is something heartbreakingly beautiful in that.

This is how life could be lived. Your presence alone, unexplained, unadvertised, brings ease to those around you. Not by trying. Not by performing goodness. Just by being. People soften. Animals trust. Even plants seem to lean in.

And when death finally arrives, it won't have to drag you kicking and screaming. It will take you gently, almost respectfully. And you will go with a smile, grateful to have existed.

You see, only humans audit existence.

Marx would point this out without ceremony. He would say your existential anxiety is not a personal failure; it is an economic feature. A human unsure of why they exist is easier to manage. They will work longer hours, chase artificial goals, and confuse exhaustion with virtue. Doesn't capitalism kill the question Why am I? It repackages it into something safer.

Why am I not successful yet?

Why am I not productive enough?

Why am I behind?

Your "why" becomes a performance review.

And then Nietzsche kicks the door open and ruins everyone's comfort.

He doesn't care about your confusion. He cares about your cowardice. Because by now it should be clear: there is no script. No destiny. No permission slip waiting to be issued. Whatever you become will be your responsibility.

And that is precisely why most people run.

Nietzsche would say you don't lack purpose. You lack the courage to stand alone with it. So you borrow meanings, inherit ambitions, download identities from culture like software you never read the terms for.

Second-hand purpose is safer than authorship.

This is where seriousness sets in. Heavy. Self-important. Grim. Which is when Osho laughs.

Not politely. Not spiritually. Laughs like someone who finds the entire situation absurd. He would remind you that existence is not a problem to solve but a phenomenon to participate in. That your obsession with purpose has less to do with depth and more to do with fear.

Osho would say existence is playful. And that seriousness is the real disease. A symptom of people who have forgotten how to dance but insist on choreographing life anyway.

And just when you think you've reached clarity, Krishnamurti dismantles the entire structure quietly.

He does not answer the question.

He removes the questioner.

He would point out that the mind demanding an answer is conditioned, trained to seek security, certainty, and authority. A fearful mind cannot ask a free question. It can only demand reassurances.

And that is when all the philosophies collapse into something disturbingly simple.

They disagree violently.

They cancel each other out.

And yet all point to the same place.

Your awareness, standing naked without explanations.

The question survives because it was never meant to be answered. It was meant to keep you awake. To prevent you from sleepwalking through borrowed lives and inherited meanings. To haunt you just enough to stop you from becoming comfortable with lies.

And then, one day, you die.

No grand summary. No exit interview. No cosmic applause. Just a quiet administrative stamp somewhere in the universe.

The Great Human Sabotage of Purpose

Humans don't just fail to find purpose.

They *manufacture obstacles* to avoid it.

Here are the most common

1. The Purpose Olympics

Everyone wants the most meaningful purpose.

Nobody wants

- Quiet living,
- Gentle joy,
- Unglamorous meaning,
- Simple existence.

Everyone wants

- World-changing purpose,
- Legacy,
- Greatness,
- A biography titled *"The Man Who Defied Mediocrity and Won."*

Humanity has turned purpose into a competition.

A sport.

A bloodbath of ambition.

Your purpose must be

- Scalable,
- Instagrammable,
- Inspiring,
- Monetizable,

- And preferably ted-talk-compatible.

2. The "I Need More Time" Illusion

Humans believe they need

- More meditation,
- More journaling,
- More clarity,
- More signs from the universe,
- More YouTube videos titled *"how to find your purpose in 3 steps."*

But none of these brings you closer to the truth.

They bring you closer to delusion.

3. The "Maybe Tomorrow" Syndrome

Your purpose is always waiting for you in the future never in the inconvenient realm of now.

You will

- Start writing tomorrow,
- Change your job tomorrow,
- Begin healing tomorrow,
- Live fully tomorrow.

But tomorrow has no interest in you.

It is already busy letting other people down.

The Anti-Purpose Manifesto (Expanded)

Purpose, as sold in modern times, is a scam.

A seductive, profitable scam.

The biggest Ponzi scheme in the self-help industry.

So here's the truth bomb:

**You do not need a purpose.

You need a life. **

Purpose does not give life meaning.

Life gives purpose and meaning.

Purpose obsession is the cancer of modern consciousness.

It turns existence into

- A checklist,
- A brand,
- A productivity contest,
- A spiritual audition.

The more you chase purpose, the more purpose runs away.

Like a cat.

Or happiness.

Or your ex.

This is where Marx enters again, clearing his throat dramatically.

Your purpose has been replaced by your job description."

In capitalism, purpose becomes

- Performance,
- Productivity,
- Efficiency,
- Success metrics,
- Hustle culture,
- LinkedIn achievements.

Capitalism doesn't want you to ask "Why am I?"

It wants you to ask

- Why am I not earning more?
- Why am I not working harder?
- Why am I not progressing faster?
- Why am I not upgrading my lifestyle?

It replaces existential inquiry with economic anxiety.

If you ever sincerely asked, "Why am I?" during office hours, you would be fired before you finish the question mark.

Conversations in the Cosmic Bar-

Now imagine all these philosophers sitting in a bar at 2:44 AM.

The bartender is God, polishing glasses He doesn't own.

Camus sips wine

"Life is absurd. Drink anyway."

Kafka nervously asks

"Is this bar licensed? Are we allowed to be here?"

Aristotle says

"This bar has a purpose. Clearly."

Marx growls

"Who owns this bar? Who profits?"

Nietzsche stands on a table

"I OWN MY PURPOSE AND THIS TABLE!"

Osho sips something suspicious

"Relax. All this is just a cosmic joke."

Krishnamurti closes his eyes

"The bar is a construct. The drinker is a construct. The need to drink is a construct."

And you, poor you, sit there with your existential cocktail (Long Island Iced Tea with 400 ice cubes), thinking:

"I just wanted to know why I exist."

The philosophers stare at you.

Camus: "Because you choose to."

Kafka: "Because of an administrative error."

Aristotle: "Because nature intended it."

Marx: "Because capitalism needs labour."

Nietzsche: “Because you must become!”

Osho: “Because existence plays.”

Krishnamurti: “Because you are aware.”

And all of them are right.

And all of them are wrong.

Because the question is not theirs.

It is yours.

The Inner Labyrinth

So far, the philosophers have entertained you, confused you, contradicted each other, and left you mildly traumatised.

But none of them has solved your problem.

Because “Why am I?” is not answered in Paris cafés, ancient Greek schools, or cosmic bars.

It is answered in the Inner Labyrinth, the most terrifying piece of real estate in existence: your own mind.

This is where you discover the uncomfortable truth:

“Why am I?” is not a question about meaning.

It is a question about you.

Not the “you” you show your relatives.

Not the “you” you show online.

Not the “you” that fills forms and resumes.

But the you beneath all that,

The you that refuses to be narrated.

This is why you avoid the question.

It is easier to chase someone else's "why" than to confront your own.

The terrifying truth

The question "Why am I?" has no final answer.

But it has a direction: inward.

Every philosopher, even when contradicting each other, is pointing you back toward yourself

- Camus → Create meaning
- Kafka → Accept uncertainty
- Aristotle → Pursue excellence
- Marx → Reclaim your selfhood
- Nietzsche → Become yourself
- Osho → Celebrate existence
- Krishnamurti → Observe without judgment

All of them disagree.

All of them argue.

All of them shout over each other.

But all of them, accidentally or inevitably,

Lead to the same door:

Your consciousness.

"Why am I?" is not answered in the labyrinth.

It *is* the labyrinth.

And walking it consciously is the purpose.

Living the Question

By now, the philosophers have yelled, argued, smoked, smirked, contradicted each other, and left you existentially disoriented.

You've travelled through absurdity, bureaucracy, teleology, capitalism, freedom, meaning, and consciousness.

And now the question sits before you again:

Why am I?

But it feels different now.

Lighter.

More intimate.

Less like a cosmic interrogation and more like a whisper from within.

This is where we stop thinking about the question and begin learning how to live it.

How to Live When Meaning Isn't Required

Living precedes meaning.

Meaning does NOT precede living.

You do not wait for purpose before living.

You live, and purpose emerges like fragrance from motion.

So how do you live the question?

1. Live With Awareness (Not Answers)

Awareness is the secret sauce nobody wants to admit is the entire meal.

Awareness does not require

- Enlightenment,
- Meditation,
- Chanting,
- Retreats,
- Himalayan caves,
- Breathing exercises that make you dizzy.

Awareness simply means

"You see yourself clearly."

When you live with awareness

- You see your desires without worshipping them,
- You see your fears without running from them,
- You see your habits without defending them,
- You see your conditioning without collapsing into it.

Awareness is the quiet miracle.

Osho would call it *witnessing*.

Krishnamurti would call it *choiceless observation.*

Nietzsche would call it *self-creation.*

You can call it whatever you want — as long as you do it.

2. Live With Joy (Not Just Survival)

Joy is not a luxury.

Joy is not optional.

Joy is not a reward at the end of achievement.

Joy is the point.

Imagine a squirrel.

Does it look burdened by purpose?

Does it appear tortured by the cosmic weight of existence?

Does it fear that its contribution to society is insufficient?

No.

The squirrel jumps, eats, steals your snacks, and enjoys existence.

Joy is the most natural state of consciousness.

Suffering is the unnatural one.

This is why Nietzsche argues for the Yes-sayer, the human who says "Yes" to life, not with blind optimism but with creative courage.

This is why Osho insists that seriousness is a spiritual disease.

This is why Camus ends *The Myth of Sisyphus* by saying:

"One must imagine Sisyphus happy."

Humanity has forgotten that joy is not the outcome. It is the raw material.

3. Live Creatively (In Any Form)

Creation is not limited to art.

You create when you

- Build a business,
- Cook a meal,
- Have a conversation,
- Decorate your room,
- Solve a problem,
- Raise a child,
- Write an email with more love than necessary,
- Help someone who can never repay you,
- Take a step toward a life that feels like yours.

Creation is the antidote to nihilism.

The universe creates endlessly.

Why shouldn't you?

4. Live Kindly (A Great Purpose in Disguise)

If you want a purpose, here is one:

"Leave people better than you found them."

That alone qualifies as a spiritual mission, a moral compass, a life philosophy.

Kindness is not sentimental.

It is revolutionary.

And it is the only thing that will be remembered after you die.

Not your achievements.

Not your salary.

Not your degrees.

Not your followers.

But the way you made people feel.

5. Live Without Pretending

Here is the greatest tragedy of modern life:

Humans pretend so hard to be someone that they forget how to be themselves.

Every day you perform roles

- Employee,
- Citizen,
- Family member,
- Achiever,
- Spiritual aspirant,
- “Valuable member of society."

Pretending becomes a full-time job.

Authenticity becomes a secret hobby.

"It is no measure of health to be well-adjusted to a profoundly sick society." (Krishnamurthy)

Living without pretending is not rebellion,

it is sanity.

***

Death: The Final Clarifier

Now let's talk about death.

Your favourite topic. (Sorry, mine)

The one you avoid while pretending you don't avoid it.

Death is the most honest philosopher.

Death doesn't care about

- Your legacies,
- Your trophies,
- Your career progressions,
- Your unlocking-your-potential workshops,
- Your self-optimisation routines,
- Your top 10 morning habits of billionaires.

Death asks only one question

"Did you live?"

Seneca, the Stoic, wrote

"It is not that we have a short time to live, but that we waste a lot of it."

The moment you face death honestly,

"Why am I?" becomes clearer.

Not because death gives you answers,

But because it removes the nonsense.

Death wipes out

- Fear of judgment,
- Obsession with success,
- Need for validation,
- Inherited expectations,
- Societal pressures.

What remains is the only thing that ever mattered:

Awareness.

Joy.

Kindness.

Presence.

Courage.

Freedom.

Death clarifies life by stripping away everything that isn't living.

Everything you search for

Is never out there.

It is always in the way you live.

Chapter - 8
Love and Other Things

Love, contrary to centuries of poetry and Bollywood misinformation, is not something you *hold on to*.

It is something that arrives politely, rearranges your furniture, sets fire to your emotional curtains, and then leaves with half your dignity in a reusable bag.

Love is not a possession.

Love is a temporary disturbance.

Everyone thinks love is about togetherness, commitment, merging of souls, two bodies one heart, blah blah spiritual nonsense. No. Real love is about letting go of yourself, your ego, your façade, your sense of being in control. It strips you, exposes you, softens you, terrifies you. It doesn't make you whole; it makes you hollow in all the right (and wrong) places.

And then comes the irony:

Love also makes you selfish.

Not the charming "I want the best for us" is selfish.

The embarrassing, needy, "Why didn't you text back in 17 minutes?" selfish.

Love demands expectation.

Expectation demands disappointment.

Disappointment demands drama.

Drama demands apologies.

Apologies demand repetition.

Repetition demands therapy.

And people keep calling this beautiful.

The funniest part is that love's original sin is not betrayal—it's predictability. Once love becomes familiar, routine, expected… it stops being love. And humans have a talent for taking love for granted.

This is why marriage, our grand cultural monument to "forever," is now a rotting institution. Not because people are immoral, but because love was never built for long-term storage.

Love is a shapeshifter.

It moves.

It mutates.

It gets bored with its own intensity.

It craves novelty like a child.

But society insists you must anchor love permanently to one individual, in one house, under one set of rituals, until one of you dies, or wishes to.

So people stay.

Not because the love remains, but because the memory of love remains. They cling to the shards, hoping the original sensation will reboot like an old laptop. It won't. Once love changes form, it never returns to factory settings.

And yet staying becomes moral, leaving becomes sin, and seeking what you lost becomes scandal.

This is why extra-marital affairs flourish like wildflowers in the cracks of domestic boredom. It's not degeneracy. It's biology plus psychology plus a dash of delusion. Humans want love to behave like a loyal dog.

Love behaves more like a stray cat, affectionate when it chooses, gone when it chooses.

The tragedy is not that love leaves.

The tragedy is that we expect it to stay.

Love's true nature is not eternal companionship.

It is **a well-wisher**, a force that shapes you, softens you, bruises you, expands you, and then leaves once its work is done. Love is not your soulmate. It is your teacher, your tormentor, your sculptor, your accident.

It comes with purpose.

It leaves with dignity.

We are the ones who cling like emotional barnacles.

We romantic fools want permanence from a phenomenon that is literally built on impermanence.

So let go of yourself.

Not for spiritual enlightenment, not because some guru on YouTube told you to "release your inner child," but because holding on to your own misery is a full-time job and the salary is pathetic.

Let go, and you'll notice something strange: grief also loosens its grip. It doesn't vanish dramatically; it just gets bored. Grief is like an audience—if you stop performing, it stops clapping.

All those nights of sulking in a dark corner, scrolling through old photos, stalking their Instagram, over-analysing texts from 2021—those weren't love. That was just the echo of a void forming inside you, a hollow space where certainty used to live.

And that's fine.

Voids are important.

Voids mean there is finally space for something real.

Because now you can fill the emptiness with things that are actually yours.

Travel without being interrogated.

Dance without being evaluated.

Enrol in that DJ class and mix tracks terribly, without someone rolling their eyes or asking if it's "midlife crisis or new hobby."

And just when you start enjoying this new freedom, when you begin to feel like a single-person festival, love will return. Uninvited, unannounced, unnecessarily dramatic.

Because love is a sadist.

A beautifully dressed, emotionally gifted sadist.

It enjoys watching you rebuild just enough to topple you again. It knows your weak spots because it created them. So yes, love will come back, wearing a different face, speaking gentler words, pretending to have matured.

And you, poor optimist, will think

This time, I know better. This time, I am wiser. This time, I won't fall so easily.

Which is cute.

Because soon enough, boom! Everything collapses again.

Everything you trusted, everything you carefully stitched back together, everything you dared to believe in, it all crumbles like a pack of cards built on hope and blind optimism.

But don't panic.

You knew this could happen.

Life isn't unfair; it's just honest.

This is the beauty of living: it teaches you to suffer gracefully and emerge tougher, not hardened, just more aware.

But listen closely

Do *not* become bitter.

Do *not* transform heartbreak into personality.

Do *not* swear off love like a drunk man swears off alcohol "forever."

And for heaven's sake

- Do not join a spiritual retreat to "heal your heart,"
- Do not force yourself into meditation just because your heart is broken,
- And definitely do not join a gym in a fit of rage, thinking a six-pack will compensate for emotional bankruptcy.

Let your heart break cleanly, not theatrically.

Because despite every disaster, every disappointment, every false beginning, you must allow love to return. And it will. Not because you chased it, not because you deserve it, but because love is stubborn and strangely loyal.

Someday, without warning, you will stumble upon someone who loves you for you, not your money, not your degrees, not your prestige, not your carefully managed social image. Someone who sees you fully and chooses you anyway.

Someone who stays.

Through thick, thin, and the occasional stupidity.

Someone for whom loving you is not a project, but a privilege.

Yes, it will happen.

But not before love tests you.

Not before life humbles you, quietly, slowly, thoroughly.

Humility brings acceptance.

Acceptance brings patience.

Patience brings clarity.

And clarity is the only thing that helps when life feels foggy and sad and uncooperative. Because someday, in your old age, when your knees betray you, but your memory still works, you will sit with yourself and replay everything, not the achievements, not the promotions, not the applause, but the *moments* you ran away from.

What you will miss most are the things you could have done differently.

The risks you avoided.

The truths you swallowed.

The chances you never took because someone else's expectations felt heavier than your own desires.

Palliative care professionals have said this for decades:

The greatest regret of the dying is painfully simple-

"I didn't dare to live a life true to myself. Instead, I lived the life others expected of me."

Imagine realising that when the curtain is already falling.

What's the point of enlightenment after the show is over?

So, friends, love freely.

Recklessly.

Generously.

With nothing to ask in return.

Absolutely nothing.

Because love given freely cannot disappoint you.

Only expectations can.

And when you realise, gently, honestly, that love has completed its course in your life, that its presence has turned into weight, that its warmth has become exhaustion…

Walk away with dignity.

Do not cling.

Do not bargain.

Do not negotiate.

Leave before love starts consuming you.

Leave before your heart becomes collateral.

Leave because you understand that some endings are not tragedies,

They are released.

And release is also a form of love.

Children leave their parents to pursue their dreams, goals, whatever. They leave their parents to such an extent that they do not return to them even when they are dying. Why? Because parents are no longer useful.

Because careers are at stake.

Because business deals must close.

Because deadlines must be met.

What a purposeful life!!!

Now imagine the reverse.

Imagine your parents had walked away from *you* when you were helpless, feverish, terrified.

Imagine they had said,

"Sorry, beta, big meeting tomorrow. Good luck with the chickenpox."

Your entire façade of strength would disintegrate instantly.

Every privilege, every comfort, every stable bone in your body exists because someone, once upon a time, sacrificed their time, money, sleep, mental health, and personal ambitions so you could breathe easily.

And yet, when the roles shift, we suddenly develop amnesia.

We forget the hands that built us.

We forget the nights they didn't sleep so we could.

We forget that our independence was sponsored.

And then, after abandoning them, we want to be "good parents" ourselves. How adorable.

Because here's the joke:

Your child is watching you.

Not God.

Not the universe.

Not karma.

Your own child.

They are learning abandonment from the master.

They are studying your emotional economics.

They are memorising your priorities.

And one day, with chilling efficiency, they will return the favour.

Not out of malice.

Not out of cruelty.

Simply because you taught them how.

And in that moment, when the loneliness you once outsourced finally comes home,

You will realise, painfully and clearly,

That it was always you who needed to change.

So try, really try, to be a good child to your parents.

And by "good," I do not mean sending gifts once a year, forwarding WhatsApp quotes, or calling them only when you are stuck in traffic and have nothing else to do.

I mean a child who understands timing.

A child who knows when it's time to *stop everything*, the ambition, the deadlines, the theatrics of adulthood, and go home.

A child who returns when their parents' steps slow down, when their eyesight fades, when their world shrinks to a few rooms and a few memories.

Be the kind of child who shows up.

Not out of obligation, but out of recognition, that these are the people who built your foundation inch by inch, night by night, with no applause and no expectation.

Serve them in their final years.

Not because you owe them (though you do),

But because doing so is one of the last acts of pure love left in this noisy, transactional world.

A child who prioritises the comfort of ageing parents over the vanity of career milestones, this is a life worth living. Because at the end, when your own breath becomes shallow, and your own regrets start knocking, you won't be haunted by the question:

"Why wasn't I there?"

Instead, you will carry a quiet, radiant certainty:

You showed up.

You held their hands.

You softened their ending.

You honoured the people who spent their best years making sure you survived your beginning.

When your own end nears, you will smile, not because life was perfect, but because you didn't abandon the ones who never abandoned you. That small truth will warm your pillow more than any legacy, achievement, or bank balance ever could.

You will be a happy person in your final days,

or at least a deeply content one.

And contentment, at the end of life, is the rarest form of wealth.

Sex, Desire, and the Performance of Intimacy

Sex used to be an instinct.

Now it's a committee decision.

Somewhere between therapy jargon and Instagram intimacy coaches, sex stopped being something you *fell into* and became something you *prepared for*. You don't just undress anymore, you negotiate. You don't desire, you check in. You don't surrender, you communicate.

Desire, once wild and irresponsible, is now on probation.

Modern intimacy demands that sex be emotionally intelligent, mutually affirming, trauma-informed, consent-checked, expectation-aligned, and preferably scheduled after dinner but before existential dread sets in. By the time all conditions are satisfied, desire has politely excused itself and gone to watch Netflix.

Sex today is rarely about hunger.

It's about reassurance. It's about you feeling empowered. It's about getting your chakras aligned.

"Do you still find me attractive?"

"Are we okay?"

"Was that good for you?"

"Should we talk about what just happened?"

Nothing kills arousal faster than a post-coital performance review.

We've turned sex into a service industry. Intimacy comes with invisible invoices. Affection is extended on credit. Desire is conditional upon consistency, validation, and long-term emotional forecasts.

But desire hates predictability.

Desire thrives on mystery.

Intimacy thrives on safety.

Modern relationships demand both, simultaneously, and then blame each other when neither survives.

We confuse closeness with ownership. We believe knowing everything about someone will deepen intimacy. Instead, it removes curiosity. When nothing is left to discover, desire quietly packs its bags and leaves without a goodbye note.

And then we panic.

We read articles.

Listen to podcasts.

Attend workshops.

Talk. Talk. Talk.

We communicate the desire for death.

By the time sex happens, it feels like a rehearsed play. Everyone knows their lines. Everyone is present. Nobody is lost. Nobody is surprised. Nobody is reckless enough to forget themselves.

Which brings us to the uncomfortable truth

Most people are not bored with sex. They are bored with predictability masquerading as maturity. Where is the mystery? Where is the teasing? The difference between us humans and animals having sex is that we can have sex for pleasure!!! Isn't that a great blessing??? But what do we do instead? We perform sex. We do it in a way that feels more like a job than a pleasure.

Marriage, Monogamy, and the Sacred Art of Being Bored Together

Marriage is society's boldest gamble: the belief that desire can be institutionalised.

It promises forever to something that was never designed for permanence. It expects passion to survive routine, mortgages, shared bathrooms, and the slow erosion of mystery caused by seeing the same person every day in bad lighting.

Monogamy isn't the villain.

Unexamined expectation is.

Marriage often begins as love and slowly turns into logistics. Who will buy groceries? Who forgot to pay the bill? Who sighed louder during dinner? Desire becomes collateral damage in the war of responsibilities.

Boredom sets in, not because love has died, but because novelty has been outlawed.

We expect one person to be our lover, best friend, emotional anchor, therapist, adventure partner, intellectual equal, sexual fantasy, and spiritual companion, for decades (or, when we don't have an option, or options, or whatever). And when they fail (as they must), we call it a crisis.

Marriage didn't fail.

Your expectations did.

Marriage doesn't kill love.

It kills the illusion that love can remain unchanged.

And boredom?

Boredom isn't the enemy.

Refusing to acknowledge it is.

So people stay. Not because desire remains, but because history does. Because leaving feels immoral. Because staying feels responsible. Because boredom is socially acceptable, but longing is suspicious.

And then come the affairs.

Not always driven by lust. Often driven by the intoxicating feeling of being *wanted without explanation*. Of being desired without having to perform familiarity. Of being seen anew.

Extra-marital affairs aren't always about sex. They're about escaping the weight of being known too well. When the expectations outweigh warmth, marriages crumble. To remain married is a brave thing to do, but to come out of it is the wise thing to do. I say this in all honesty (and all humour) that Marriage, I often say, is like walking into a lion's den.

No one pushes you in. You walk in willingly, either because you're blind, hopelessly optimistic, or genuinely incapable of identifying a lion's den even when it has a signboard.

Now, here's the part people usually misunderstand.

If the lion is married, things get interesting. Because the lioness has already done her work. She has turned the king of the jungle into a well-behaved dog, house-trained, emotionally conditioned, and responsive to tone.

And by the time you decide to leave the den, congratulations, you are one too.

Two dogs walk out together.

One former lion.

One former free human.

Both obedient.

Both domesticated.

Both were pretending this was always the plan.

From the lioness's point of view, she is busy raising the kids, doing most of the hunting, performing sex (as a duty) and quietly praying for a new lion to claim the throne (we are strictly talking about lions here). Also, the lioness does get horny occasionally, but finds the lion busy stalking other lionesses, and so she slowly descends back to her prayer. This was not necessarily for lions (contradicting ourselves, are we). In all fairness, being a lioness is tough as hell. She has to protect herself and the kids from getting beaten up, and the occasional love that comes her way. On the other hand, most monkeys are unapologetically polygamous.

With a few loyal exceptions, titi monkeys and owl monkeys, the romantic poets of the primate world, everyone else in the monkey family treats monogamy like a weekend experiment that failed.

They mate freely, opportunistically, without guilt, vows, or anniversary dinners. No promises are made. None are broken. No one asks, *"Where is this going?"* The answer is obvious: forward, briefly, and then elsewhere.

And before we get offended, remember: we are their descendants. Slightly overdressed apes with bills and stress.

Our predatory ancestors didn't survive ice ages by lighting candles and committing forever. They survived by diluting risk. Polygamy wasn't rebellion; it was insurance. More mates meant more offspring. More offspring meant better odds that *someone* would survive the winter, the famine, the neighbouring tribe with sharper sticks.

Monogamy, back then, wasn't moral superiority. It was a logistical inconvenience.

Evolution didn't select for loyalty.

It was selected for survival.

So when modern humans feel restless inside lifelong exclusivity, it's not necessarily a character flaw. It's ancient software running on a very new operating system, one that insists on commitment contracts, emotional transparency, and joint bank accounts.

Your DNA still remembers the forest.

Society just put it in a cubicle.

This doesn't mean everyone should run wild and blame biology for bad behaviour. That's lazy and deeply unattractive. But it does mean we should stop pretending that monogamy is the natural default and desire is a malfunction.

Desire isn't broken.

Expectation is.

Animals don't cheat.

They don't lie.

They don't promise what they can't biologically guarantee.

Only humans do that, then write poetry about the disappointment.

So yes, monkeys are polygamous.

Apes are opportunistic.

Our ancestors were pragmatic.

And we, poor, overthinking descendants, are trying to negotiate ancient instincts using marriage laws, therapy jargon, and scented candles.

It's not immoral.

It's mismatched engineering.

Monogamy, Represent!!!

Now, before biology is dragged into court as a defence lawyer, let's be clear about something.

Instinct explains desire.

It does not excuse behaviour.

Yes, we descend from polygamous primates. Yes, our ancestors survived through opportunistic bonding. Yes, novelty excites us in ways routine never will. All of this is true, and still completely insufficient as justification.

Because evolution gave us urges, not instructions.

What separates humans from monkeys is not morality; it is choice. A conscious choice. And this choice, inconveniently, comes with restraint. Not repression. Not denial. Restraint. The conscious ability to pause, observe desire, and decide whether acting on it aligns with the life you want to live.

Animals don't choose.

They respond.

Humans respond, and then write books like this explaining why they *had* to.

Restraint is not anti-pleasure. It is anti-impulse. It is the difference between desire as experience and desire as compulsion. Without restraint, desire stops being erotic and starts being repetitive. Predictable. Empty.

Freedom without restraint isn't liberation.

It's just restlessness with better excuses.

Choosing monogamy, then, is not a denial of nature, it's a deliberate stance against clutter. Some people choose it because it offers depth over breadth. Because staying allows something rarer to develop: familiarity without contempt, closeness without ownership, desire that matures instead of combusts.

Others choose non-monogamy, not as indulgence, but as honesty, because pretending otherwise would be more damaging than restraint ever could be.

The keyword here is *choice.*

Not compulsion.

Not entitlement.

Not biology dressed as destiny.

Restraint is not about suppressing desire. It's about not being enslaved by it. It's the difference between wanting something and *needing* it to feel alive.

The tragedy isn't desire wandering.

The tragedy is never questioning why it wanders, and blindly following wherever it points.

You don't become mature by killing desire.

You become mature by not letting desire run your life like a drunk driver.

So no, this is not an argument for chaos.

It's an argument for honesty.

Honesty about who we are.

Honesty about what we want.

And honesty about what we are willing, and unwilling, to live with.

Anything else is just instinct pretending to be philosophy.

And monkeys, for all their wisdom, have never claimed enlightenment.

Humans, unfortunately, have.

We believe that everything can be improved by talking about it. That clarity is always progress. That articulation is intimacy. So when desire misbehaves, when attraction wobbles, when mystery refuses to cooperate, we do what modern humans do best: we schedule a conversation

Why Communication Ruined Sex

(A Tragedy in Multiple Conversations)

Communication is wonderful.

For contracts.

For boundaries.

For conflict resolution.

It is disastrous for desire.

Sex does not want to be explained. It does not want to be dissected, optimised, or emotionally narrated. Desire is irrational. It doesn't respond well to bullet points.

Modern relationships treat communication like lubricant: the more, the better.

So we talk about sex before sex.

During sex.

After sex.

Weeks later.

In therapy.

We analyse tone. Timing. Intention. Impact.

Desire watches all this from a distance and thinks, *"Absolutely not."*

Communication turns mystery into management. It turns spontaneity into strategy. It replaces curiosity with clarity, and clarity is rarely erotic.

You don't desire someone because you understand them completely.

You desire them because something about them remains unknowable.

The moment sex becomes a topic instead of an experience, it loses its teeth.

This doesn't mean silence is the solution. It means not everything needs to be processed to death. Some moments are meant to be lived, not archived.

Sex needs room for awkwardness.

For misfires.

For misunderstandings.

For laughter.

For imperfection.

When everything must be articulated, nothing remains felt.

The cruel irony? We communicate more than ever, and touch less. We explain our needs endlessly and feel less desired. We are emotionally fluent and erotically illiterate.

Sex didn't disappear.

We talked it into submission. We had sex. We barely knew what we were doing, which falls into which category. It was raw, unhinged and unapologetically beautiful. Now we have compartmentalised sex. We are either this or that. Top or bottom. What if we want to be both? Or right or left? You want to handcuff your girlfriend, be my guest. Blindfold?? Excellent!!! But just get on with it, do not tell me what you are doing is called what. We have turned sex into meaningless desire.

And once desire is exhausted, once intimacy has been analysed to death, humans do what they have always done best when meaning collapses, they distract themselves.

With work.

With ambition.

With money.

Because if love is confusing, at least money keeps score.

Which brings us to the next compulsory subject in the curriculum of being alive.

Chapter - 9
Money Matters

Earning money is not optional. It is one of life's compulsory subjects, like heartbreak, disappointment, and taxes. Everyone has to go through it, whether they like it or not. What most people misunderstand, however, is that money is not merely a question of *how much*. It is very much a question of *how*.

Though we understand money in terms of quantity, it is actually the quality of money earned that is important. Take a bribe and see how you fare in your old age. It will haunt you like a lizard in a closet. Take a bribe and watch what happens, not immediately, of course. Corruption is patient. It waits. It shows up quietly in your old age, when distractions run out, and mirrors become honest. That money will sit beside you, hissing softly, reminding you that you sold small pieces of yourself very cheaply.

Give a bribe, and something else collapses instantly: your self-respect. It falls like a poorly constructed house of cards. You may justify it as a necessity, system, survival, or "how things work," but your spine knows the truth. It always does.

Money should be earned in such a way that on a grey, rainy morning, when the world feels heavy, and your reflection looks back at you without filters, you don't feel like absolute shit. That's the real test. Not wealth rankings. Not applause. Just whether you can meet your own eyes without flinching.

So how does one earn money without losing oneself?

It's embarrassingly simple, and therefore ignored.

Read.

Read obsessively.

Read dangerously.

Not course books. Not motivational garbage promising ten steps to becoming rich before breakfast. Read books that stretch your sense of time, patience, and proportion. Read books that teach you how to *live*, books that disturb you, slow you down, and force you to confront uncomfortable truths. Books that don't give answers, but sharpen your questions. (Yes, occasionally, books like this one.)

Educate yourself enough to recognise the difference between vanity and pride.

Vanity wants money so it can be seen.

Pride wants money so it can stand quietly.

Vanity asks, *"How do I look?"*

Pride asks, *"Can I sleep?"*

When you learn this difference, your relationship with money changes. You stop chasing it like a saviour and start treating it like a tool, useful, necessary, but not sacred.

Money matters.

But not more than you do.

And any currency earned at the cost of your dignity will charge interest later, compounded, merciless, and payable when you're too tired to negotiate.

This is also where people get confused about ambition.

Ambition itself is not the villain. Blind ambition is.

Blind ambition doesn't ask questions. It just accelerates. It justifies everything retroactively. It tells you you'll fix your ethics later, after the next promotion, after the next deal, after the next milestone. But "later" has a strange habit of never arriving.

Money earned without integrity always sends invoices downstream.

Sometimes the bill arrives as anxiety.

Sometimes as insomnia.

Sometimes as a constant need to prove yourself.

And sometimes it arrives quietly, in old age, when achievements stop distracting you, and silence becomes unavoidable.

Money matters, yes. Bills must be paid. Comfort is not a sin. Wanting stability is not a weakness. But confusing money with worth, that's where things rot.

You are not what you earn.

You are what you trade away to earn it.

If your work costs you your honesty, your time, your health, your relationships, your ability to sit quietly without panic, then you are not being paid. You are being bought.

And the tragedy is that most people don't even negotiate the price properly.

Earn money. Earn it well. Earn it cleanly. Earn it in ways that don't require elaborate justifications at dinner tables or moral gymnastics in your head.

Because when everything else is stripped away, titles, relevance, applause, what remains is a simple question:

Was the life you financed worth the cost?

Entrepreneurship, when stripped of Instagram filters and pitch-deck poetry, is one of the most fearless ways to earn money. Not because it guarantees success—God no—but because it removes the most dangerous illusion of all: **someone else will take responsibility for your life**.

Entrepreneurship gives you freedom, yes. But not the cheap, motivational-poster kind of freedom. Not the "work from the beach" fantasy sold by people who have never run payroll. It gives you a heavier freedom—the kind that comes with consequences.

You are free to decide.

And therefore, free to fail.

You are free to dream.

And therefore, fully accountable when the dream collapses at 3 a.m.

Entrepreneurship does not babysit you. It does not provide emotional cushioning. It does not offer severance packages for bad decisions. It exposes you—financially, psychologically, ethically.

And that is precisely why it is honest.

A job can hide many things. It can hide mediocrity behind systems. It can hide cowardice behind hierarchy. It can hide resentment behind monthly salaries. Entrepreneurship hides nothing. Your results walk naked into the room every single day.

If your business survives, it is because you showed up.

If it fails, it is because you misjudged something.

The market does not care about your intentions, your effort, or your trauma.

And strangely, this brutality is liberating.

Because entrepreneurship breaks the false separation between **freedom and accountability**. Most people want freedom without responsibility and responsibility without freedom. Entrepreneurship gives you both, tightly coupled, non-negotiable.

You are free, but you are answerable.

You are independent, but you are exposed.

You are powerful, but you are not protected.

This does something important to your character.

You stop blaming systems.

You stop outsourcing failures.

You stop waiting for permission.

You learn humility faster than any spiritual practice ever could. Nothing dissolves ego like a customer who refuses to buy. Nothing teaches clarity like cash flow. Nothing sharpens ethics like knowing that every dishonest rupee earned will return as chaos later.

Entrepreneurship also forces you to confront money honestly.

There is no fixed paycheck to anaesthetize you. No HR department to moralise your discomfort. Every rupee you earn has a visible origin. You know who paid you. You know why. And if they stop paying, you know exactly where to look at yourself, your value, your relevance.

This kind of earning builds dignity.

Not arrogance. Not entitlement. Dignity.

Because you are not paid for time spent pretending. You are paid for value created. Real value. Something someone else voluntarily exchanges money for, not because a system forced them to, but because they found it useful.

Entrepreneurship, when done cleanly, also keeps your conscience intact. You cannot afford prolonged self-deception. You cannot lie to yourself for too long; the numbers won't allow it. Reality intervenes quickly.

That's why entrepreneurship, at its best, produces adults.

Not in age, but in responsibility.

You learn to live without guarantees.

You learn to take risks without recklessness.

You learn to stand alone without becoming lonely.

You also learn something deeply philosophical:

Freedom is not comfort.

Freedom is exposure.

Freedom is uncertainty.

Freedom is standing by your decisions when there is no one left to blame.

And yet, paradoxically, entrepreneurship gives you something priceless: the ability to look at your money without shame. To know how it was earned. To sleep without mental footnotes. To face the mirror on a rainy morning without explaining yourself.

Entrepreneurship is not for everyone. Nor should it be. Some people prefer predictability. Some need structure. Some thrive in systems. That is not a failure.

But for those who choose it, not as a shortcut to wealth, but as a way of living, it becomes a deeply human act.

You earn.

You fail.

You learn.

You adapt.

You grow.

And whatever happens, the life you finance is undeniably your own.

That alone makes entrepreneurship one of the most honest conversations a person can have with existence.

Now, before entrepreneurship starts feeling like a spiritual path with balance sheets, let's pause. Because when entrepreneurship goes wrong, it doesn't just fail; it gets a documentary.

Take Pablo Escobar.

Yes, yes, drug lord, criminal, violence, tragedy. All true. But if you strip away the illegality (just for a second, relax), what remains is an entrepreneur with frightening efficiency. Supply chains are smoother than most FMCG companies. Distribution networks that governments would envy. Brand recognition is so strong that people still wear his face on T-shirts.

Escobar wasn't short on innovation.

He was short on conscience.

Which is a small detail people often forget when worshipping "scale."

His problem wasn't ambition; it was ego on steroids. He didn't create value; he extracted it violently and called it empire-building. And like all ego-driven enterprises, it collapsed under its own weight, taking half a country's sanity along with it.

Same pattern. Different font.

You don't need cartels to see this today. You'll find modern Escobars in hoodies, calling themselves founders, preaching hustle while quietly hollowing out their teams. They speak of vision while normalising burnout. They call exploitation "passion" and exhaustion "culture."

Entrepreneurship stops being liberating the moment it becomes a personality trait.

You can spot it early. The founder who starts every sentence with "When *I* built this company…" The one who believes suffering automatically qualifies them for sainthood. The one who thinks paying people on time is generosity, not basic decency.

This is where entrepreneurship mutates, from courage into entitlement.

Risk-taking becomes moral superiority. Growth becomes justification. "I sacrificed everything" becomes a free pass to sacrifice everyone else.

And then comes scale, the silent villain.

Entrepreneurship begins as a conversation: *Here's a problem. Here's a solution.* But as it grows, it becomes an abstraction. People turn into headcount. Stories turn into metrics. Consequences turn into PowerPoint slides.

Layoffs become "realignments."

Pay cuts become "strategic recalibration."

Burnout becomes "not a culture fit."

And the founder, once brave, now insulated, sits behind dashboards, calling this leadership.

At this point, entrepreneurship isn't about freedom anymore.

It's about control with better branding.

And here's the funniest tragedy of all: the founder who wanted freedom ends up trapped. Trapped in their own creation. Trapped in quarterly expectations. Trapped in relevance anxiety. Trapped in the identity of "entrepreneur", they can't remove without feeling naked.

Escobar couldn't walk away.

Many modern founders can't either, though their prisons have glass walls, investor meetings, and flattering magazine covers.

True entrepreneurship requires something rarer than courage: **restraint**.

The ability to stop.

The humility to say, "This growth costs too much."

The discipline to remain answerable, not just to investors, but to the mirror.

Because the moment entrepreneurship loses its ethical spine, it becomes indistinguishable from the systems it once claimed to disrupt, just louder and better dressed.

So yes, entrepreneurship can be fearless.

It can be dignified.

It can be freeing.

Freedom without conscience is just another form of slavery, this time with your own logo on the gate.

Lastly

You May Now Forget This Book

If you are still reading, I should probably apologize.

Not because you wasted time - time was going to waste itself anyway, but because you reached the end expecting something. A conclusion. A final insight. A neatly folded takeaway you could place gently into your life and feel slightly superior about.

That was never the deal.

Books like this are not meant to be completed. They are meant to be abandoned halfway through, forgotten on shelves, rediscovered years later with mild embarrassment, and then quietly forgiven. Finishing it only proves one thing: you are very good at following things to their logical end, even when logic was never invited.

So let me save you some effort.

You do not need any guidance. You don't need enlightenment. You are beautifully you.

If enlightenment were necessary, existence would have made it mandatory. It didn't. Babies arrive unenlightened. Trees grow unenlightened. Dogs live and die without ever once wondering if they have "arrived." And yet, somehow, life continues, thriving, chaotic, unnecessary, beautiful.

Enlightenment has become another achievement, another badge, another way of feeling subtly incomplete. Another hill to climb, so you can look down and reassure yourself that at least you're trying. But life does not require illumination to be lived. It requires presence. Even that, imperfectly.

You don't need answers.

Answers are overrated. They are suspiciously confident. They arrive too quickly and stay too long. Most answers end conversations; they rarely deepen them. The most honest moments of living, grief, love, awe, fear arrive without explanations and leave without apologies.

You asked questions not because answers were missing, but because certainty felt safer than silence. This book didn't give you answers for the same reason life doesn't: they would have gotten in the way.

You also don't need this book anymore.

It has served its purpose by slowly becoming unnecessary. If any sentence here tries to settle into belief, gently escort it out. If any idea feels comforting, distrust it slightly. If something resonated deeply, forget it first. Whatever is real will return on its own.

Books are ladders. You climb, you see a bit more, and then, if you're wise, you stop carrying the ladder around, announcing how high you've climbed.

And finally, living is enough.

Not productive living.

Not meaningful living.

Not optimised, purposeful, spiritually curated living.

Just living.

Waking up. Drinking tea. Missing buses. Loving badly. Laughing at the wrong moment. Sitting quietly when there is nothing to fix. Being ordinary without apology. Being kind without witnesses. Being confused without rushing to clarity.

That is not a consolation prize.

That is the whole thing.

There is no final instruction. No moral. No post-credit scene where the universe explains itself. The book ends here, not because something has been completed, but because nothing ever needed completion.

You may now forget this book.

And return, without urgency, without guilt, to your own beautifully unremarkable life.